DATE DUE

Tinker v. *Des Moines* and Students' Right to Free Speech

Debating Supreme Court Decisions

Stephanie Sammartino McPherson

Enslow Publishers, Inc.
40 Industrial Road
Box 398
Berkeley Heights, NJ 07922
USA

http://www.enslow.com

For my husband, Dick.

Library of Congress Cataloging-in-Publication Data

McPherson, Stephanie Sammartino.
    Tinker v. Des Moines and students' right to free speech : debating Supreme Court decisions / Stephanie Sammartino McPherson.
        p. cm. — (Debating Supreme Court decisions)
    Includes bibliographical references and index.
    ISBN 0-7660-2538-1
    1. Tinker, John Frederick—Trials, litigation, etc. 2. Des Moines Independent Community School District—Trials, litigation, etc. 3. Freedom of speech—United States. 4. Students—Civil rights—United States. I. Title. II. Series.
    KF228.T56M37 2006
    342.7308'53—dc22

                              2006011738

Printed in the United States of America

10 9 8 7 6 5 4 3 2 1

Illustration Credits: AP/Wide World, pp. 91, 95, 102; Bettman/CORBIS, p. 10; Des Moines Register, p. 49; courtesy of Christopher Eckhardt, p. 20; Getty Images, p. 6; Harris & Ewing/Collection of the Supreme Court of the United States, p. 57; Hemera Image Express, p. 2; National Archives and Records Administration, pp. 28, 34; National Geographic Society/Collection of the Supreme Court of the United States, p. 73; St. Louis Post-Dispatch, p. 85.

Cover Illustrations: Background, Artville; photograph, Drake Mabry, copyright 1965, the Des Moines Register and Tribune Company, reprinted with permission.

Contents

Author's Note

In reconstructing the events of over forty years ago, I've found that people remember the details of the armband protest, which led to *Tinker* v. *Des Moines*, slightly differently. I have reconciled differences whenever possible and attempted to present an unbiased and accurate account.

I would like to give very special thanks to John Tinker, Mary Beth Tinker, Lorena Jeanne Tinker, and Christopher Eckhardt for sharing their recollections and feelings about the armband protest and the *Tinker* v. *Des Moines* court case. Their input contributed greatly to my understanding of events. I would also like to thank Bruce Clark for discussing the protest with me and helping me sort through details. Thank you also to Richard McPherson and Marion and Angelo Sammartino for reading the manuscript and offering suggestions.

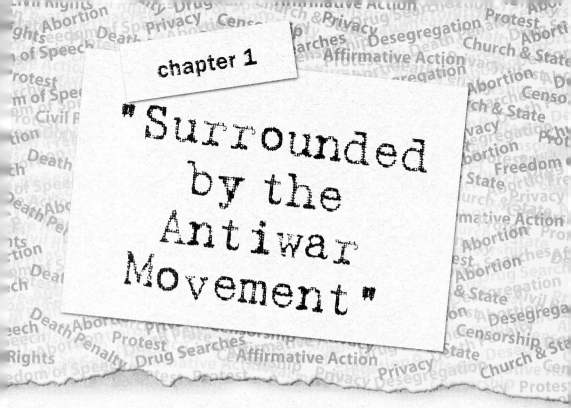

chapter 1

"Surrounded by the Antiwar Movement"

Fifteen-year-old John Tinker had never seen such an enormous crowd. Over twenty thousand strong, the masses of people stretched through Washington, D.C., on their way to the White House. It was an overwhelming experience for John.

But something impressed John more than sheer numbers. "They all agreed with me about the war," he recalled forty years later. "I was used to being in the minority. Suddenly there was this whole crowd that agreed with me."[1]

It was November 1965, and the United States had begun to step up the war in Vietnam. President Lyndon Johnson thought that it was important to help the South Vietnamese defeat the

This demonstration in Washington, D.C., was held in November 1965. John Tinker, Christopher Eckhardt, and their fellow marchers believed strongly that American involvement in Vietnam should end.

Communist North Vietnamese. Tens of thousands of American troops poured into the small Southeast Asian country. Bombs were dropped on the Communist areas.

John and his fellow protesters were marching for peace. They came from all over the country. John had arrived with a busload of students and adults from Des Moines, Iowa. Some of the marchers carried signs, but they were strangely quiet for such a large group.[2] This was not a time for shouting or rowdy behavior. U.S. servicemen and innocent Vietnamese civilians were dying.

The son of a Methodist minister, John Tinker had grown up hearing all about the peace movement and about civil rights. His antiwar stand was deep and well-considered. Even as a small child, he refused to fight with other children. "Our family was surrounded by the anti-war movement," he said, ". . . all of the kids were swept up by it."[3]

When John's mother, Lorena Jeanne Tinker, decided to attend the peace march, John immediately said he wanted to go too. For John, taking part in peace activities was as natural as "some other kid going to a band concert."[4]

John's friend from his church youth group, Christopher Eckhardt, also found it natural to oppose the war. He too had parents who were dedicated to peace and civil rights. As he walked toward the Washington Monument, Christopher hoisted a sign reading, "Follow the Geneva Courts of 1954."[5] That meant that the United States should accept the division of Vietnam that had been made at a peace conference in Geneva, Switzerland. The conference had also called for elections. If these elections were held in a way that was fair, the United States would have no reason to fight.

Both John and Christopher had other interests besides peace and civil rights. John, a sophomore at North High School in Des Moines, was an excellent musician who played the sousaphone and the violin. Christopher, a former student body president in elementary school and junior high, attended Roosevelt High School. He ran on the track team and had won trophies for weight lifting and fishing. He also delivered newspapers and had a business mowing lawns in the summer and shoveling snow in the winter.

But that day in Washington, D.C., nothing was more important to both boys than stopping the war. Riding the bus home with other young Des Moines protesters, John and Christopher joined the discussion about what they could do. Like the other college and high school students, they wanted to express their feelings in a meaningful way. They wanted to make others question whether the United States was justified in sending troops to a country that had not threatened Americans in any way.

One of the passengers on the bus had heard of a national movement to wear black armbands. John and Christopher liked the suggestion. A traditional symbol of mourning, armbands seemed a quiet but powerful way to convey an antiwar message. But the protest had to be organized. A peace meeting was scheduled at

Christopher's house. Two students from Roosevelt High School, Bruce Clark and Ross Peterson, took the lead in organizing the armband protest. Although they had not attended the peace march in Washington, both boys were deeply committed to ending the war.

The blustery afternoon of December 11, Christopher divided his time between the meeting and shoveling snow off the sidewalks. Busy with a school rehearsal, John was not able to attend the meeting. But he soon learned what had been decided.

A Bold Move

The student protesters would begin wearing armbands on December 16. They hoped to convey two messages. First, the armbands would express sorrow for all who had died in the war—both American and Vietnamese. The armbands would also show support for a Christmas Eve truce that had been suggested by Senator Robert Kennedy. If enough people backed the truce, maybe it would turn into a permanent cease-fire. John thought both reasons for wearing an armband were vitally important.

Many people considered all North Vietnamese to be the enemy. "Mourning the deaths on both sides was seen as a bold move," John Tinker said, looking back on the event.[6] He knew that some Americans would consider it unpatriotic to show any sympathy for the enemy's losses. But John and other protesters considered any combat death a terrible waste and a tragedy. They wanted to mourn all who had died in the war.

John's thirteen-year-old sister, Mary Beth, had also thought a great deal about the Vietnam War. She had not been to the march in Washington, but she felt it was important to express her views. The

Mary Beth and John Tinker are shown holding the armbands they wore to protest the war in Vietnam.

protest Ross and Bruce were organizing might lead to meaningful discussions. It might encourage her classmates to question the war. Like her brother, Mary Beth wanted to do anything she could do promote peace. She decided to wear an armband too.

Disturbing the Peace?

Plans for the protest were rapidly moving forward. In an article for the Roosevelt High School newspaper, Ross explained all about the armbands. He also said that students were encouraged to fast on December 16. How long the protest lasted would depend on the government. If the United States decided to extend the Christmas truce indefinitely, the students would stop wearing armbands. If not, they would continue to wear them through the holiday season. Ross also presented an alternative for traditional New Year celebrations. Instead of going to parties, the protesters could gather in small groups to discuss ways to end the war. On January 2, another fast would be held.

Ross expected his article to go straight into the school paper. But in an unusual move, journalism teacher Donald Haley made Ross submit it to the principal. He was afraid that the controversial nature of the piece made it unsuitable for a school publication.

Charles Rowley, the principal at Roosevelt High School, had hesitations too. Like Haley, he worried that the emotionally charged issue of the Vietnam War could seriously disrupt school routine. He decided to share Ross's article with other administrators. Together, the five high school principals in Des Moines and the school district's director of secondary education, Raymond Peterson (who was not related to Ross Peterson), would decide what to do. In explaining this move to Ross, he said the school board would not allow any activity that "disturbed the peace."[7] Neither Ross nor Bruce thought that wearing an armband would disturb the peace. But Ross's article never made it into the school newspaper.

A Front-Page Story

On Wednesday, December 15, John rose early to deliver newspapers on his neighborhood route. Arriving home, he grabbed a few minutes to scan the news before school. John stared in amazement. The armband protest had made the front page! To his chagrin, John learned that armbands would not be allowed in schools after all. Raymond Peterson had issued a statement. "For the good of the school system," he declared, "we don't think this [wearing armbands] should be permitted. . . . schools are no place for demonstrations."[8]

John was in a dilemma. A fair-minded individual, he thought the school officials deserved a chance to explain their views more fully. On the other hand, John felt he had an absolute right to wear the armband. Over and over again, he considered the matter. He had only one day to decide what to do.

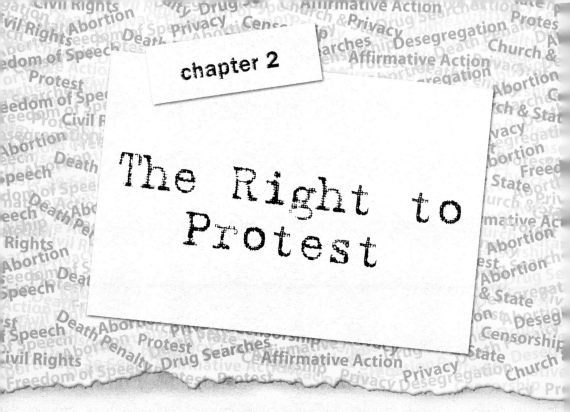

chapter 2

The Right to Protest

On Thursday morning, John still felt pulled in two directions. After delivering his papers, he began calling friends from his church youth group.[1] Some had already left for school. Others listened to John's suggestion that the protest be postponed just long enough to hear what the school officials had to say.

"I don't care," said Christopher Eckhardt, who attended the same school as Ross and Bruce. "I'm going to wear [my armband] anyway."[2] The previous day Christopher's gym teacher had declared, "Anyone who comes in with a black armband tomorrow is a Communist sympathizer. Nobody better do it."[3] Christopher was determined not to be intimidated. Mary Beth had also opted to go to school with a thin strip of black fabric circling her upper arm. John supported them completely but decided not to wear his own armband.

No one knows exactly how many students wore armbands on December 16. According to Mary Beth and Christopher, several dozen, possibly more, defied the principals' hastily made rule. Some got through the day without any problems. These included eleven-year-old Hope Tinker and eight-year-old Paul Tinker. Leonard Tinker had been a bit taken aback when he first saw his youngest children preparing to wear armbands to elementary school. "Dad, I grieve for those children in Vietnam," Hope said. "Is it wrong for me to show that I'm grieving? Isn't that what a black armband is all about?"[4] Both Hope's and Paul's teachers proved very supportive of their decisions.[5]

What Happened to Christopher

Christopher Eckhardt was not so lucky. Arriving at Roosevelt High School, Christopher went straight to the principal's office. He had decided to get the showdown with school officials over with. "You're dead!" called a member of the football team, pointing.[6] Christopher had to wait forty-five minutes for Vice Principal Donald Blackman. Asked to remove his armband, Christopher explained to Blackman that he could not comply. He believed he had a constitutional right to wear the armband.

Soon girls' adviser Velma Cross arrived and told Christopher that he was "too young to have opinions." She also warned that "colleges didn't accept protesters."[7] When Mr. Blackman asked if Christopher "was looking for a busted nose," it was the last straw.[8] Feeling bullied and helpless, Christopher began to cry. But he still refused to remove the armband. His mother, Margaret Eckhardt, backed him up. "I think he has every right to wear the armband," she replied to Mr. Blackman's phone call. "I will not ask him to take it off."[9] The vice principal then suspended Christopher from school.

What Happened to Mary Beth

Mary Beth's day at Warren Harding Junior High started off much better than Christopher's. Several classmates asked about the armband, and Mary Beth was happy to explain. At lunch several boys teased her. They said that they wanted black armbands for Christmas. But that did not bother Mary Beth.

There were no serious problems until Mary Beth got to her math class. Noting her armband, the teacher, Richard Moberly, immediately sent her to the office. Vice Principal Leo Willadsen did not seem overly concerned. He said that Mary Beth could go back to class if she took off the armband. Although she still believed in her right to wear it, Mary Beth agreed. Removing her armband, she returned to class.

Before long, however, Vera Tarmann, the girls' vice principal, came to get Mary Beth again. Ms. Tarmann explained that she understood Mary Beth's feelings. But Mary Beth had broken a school rule. Even though she had removed her armband, she had worn it for more than half a day. Ms. Tarmann said that she couldn't let her sympathy interfere with her job. She had to suspend Mary Beth.

Mary Beth recalled years later:

> I had a feeling I might get in some kind of trouble. There's a decision you have to make sometimes in life when there's a rule you don't want to follow. Many rules are there for a good reason. I felt that the rule of standing up for peace and freedom was more important [than the rule not to wear armbands.][10]

What Upset John

That evening, another meeting was held. Students who had worn armbands and students who planned to wear armbands attended with their parents. According to notes taken by John and Mary Beth's mother, Lorena Jeanne Tinker, someone had also asked a lawyer to be present. Some participants, however, believe that Craig Sawyer, an assistant professor of law at Drake University, did not become involved until later. What matters is that the armband students and their parents had a chance to meet Mr. Sawyer at some point. The following description of the meeting is taken from Mrs. Tinker's notes.

Some students felt they were being pushed to support the war at school. Bruce Clark said that one gym teacher at Roosevelt High made students chant "Beat the Vietcong" while they exercised. He intimidated those who disagreed with him, calling them "Vietnam rat finks" or "pinkos."[11]

Banning armbands seemed blatantly unfair to the students. Joe Berry, a student at Roosevelt High School, pointed out that many students had worn black armbands the year before to "mourn the death of school spirit at Roosevelt."[12] Students were also permitted to wear political campaign buttons before elections. No one worried about a clash between supporters of different candidates.

Some people hoped that the school board would settle the issue. Bruce Clark and Ross Peterson reported on a phone call they had made to the chairman of the school board, a man named Ora Niffenegger. They wanted him to call a special meeting to discuss the armband issue. "Mr. Niffenegger said he did not feel that [the] School Board should be bothered by this sort of thing," said Ross. "He tried to get across to us that this matter was not that important!"[13]

But John Tinker thought his right to protest was of vital importance. Mr. Niffenegger's attitude appalled him. "We had tried to resolve the conflict and been turned down," he recalled many years later.[14] John felt he no longer had a choice. He decided to wear an armband the very next day.

John's Protest

Rushing as usual, John arrived at North High School with scarcely a minute to spare Friday morning. He had planned to put on the armband before classes started, but there wasn't time. After his homeroom period, he went to the bathroom. Feeling slightly embarrassed, he struggled to pin on the armband. A friend had to help him attach it to his suit jacket. Usually John dressed more casually for school. But he was making a formal protest; he felt the need to look formal, too.[15]

Apprehensively, John waited for reactions from classmates and teachers. "People sometimes want to present us doing a heroic thing," he remembered in 2005. "We were kids in school and had all the anxieties and nervousness [kids] usually [have]."[16] John's tension could only grow as hours passed and no one noticed the armband! The problem was his dark suit jacket. The black armband blended right in.

After gym class, John doffed his jacket and pinned the band to his white shirt. Soon a teacher sent him to the office. John said:

> I explained to the principal that I felt I had to wear it. He was very fatherly in a way. . . . He said perhaps I didn't understand the need to support the government. . . . He was very respectful really. He talked about his wartime experiences in the Korean War.[17]

Finally, the principal, Donald M. Wetter, said, "I'll ask you to take the armband off, but I don't suppose you will."

"No, I won't," John replied.

"Then I'll have to send you home."

"I understand," said John.[18]

Christopher Eckhardt sits with his parents at a school board meeting. All three are wearing armbands, since the whole family opposed the Vietnam War.

Interest in the armband protest was growing. When John got home, he found reporters and a TV camera crew gathered at his house. John explained his feelings about the war and his belief in the right to protest.[19]

The School Board Decides

It was up to the Des Moines school board to decide what would happen next. Would armbands be allowed in school or not? Usually about twenty people attended board meetings. On December 21, 1965, two hundred people came to hear the school board's final ruling on the armbands. Craig Sawyer was also there as a representative of the Iowa Civil Liberties Union (ICLU). For two hours the board members and the public debated the issue. Finally, it was decided to postpone a decision on armbands until January. In frustration, Sawyer cried out, "Take a stand, that's what you're here for!"[20]

It wasn't until January 3, 1966, however, that the school board finally put the issue to a vote. In a 5–2 decision, they decided to uphold the rule against armbands. William Eckhardt, Christopher's father, was furious. He declared that the armbands had "started out to symbolize peace against war, but because of the reaction against them, they have taken on the further meaning of freedom against authority."[21]

chapter 3

Hawks and Doves

By the time John, Mary Beth, Christopher, Bruce, Ross, and others donned their armbands, many Americans were beginning to have doubts about the Vietnam War. They had expected a powerful nation like the United States to easily defeat the small, unorganized army of North Vietnam. But the war dragged on for many months. People began to wonder how the United States had become involved in the first place.

The roots of America's interest in Vietnam went back many years. Since the 1880s, Vietnam had been governed by France as part of French Indochina. In 1940, however, Japanese troops conquered the country. The United States denounced this action, calling for the Japanese to withdraw.

The Japanese had no intention of leaving. The Vietnamese had no intention of giving up either. They wanted their own country, and they wanted it free of French or Japanese influence. To pursue this goal, they formed the League for Independence of Vietnam, known as the Viet Minh. Although this organization was associated with the Communist party, it worked closely with the United States during World War II.

Most Americans believed that communism stood in opposition to the values of a free society. But during the war years, it was more important to defeat Japan than to limit communism. The Viet Minh provided valuable help to the U.S. war effort. Soldiers in the Viet Minh located American pilots who had been shot down and rescued Americans from Japanese prisons. They shared important information that they gleaned from their spies. The leader of the Viet Minh was a man named Ho Chi Minh. He became a special agent for the major U.S. intelligence organization.

Struggle for Independence

After the war, Ho Chi Minh declared Vietnam an independent nation. But French officials still considered their country the rightful ruler of Vietnam. They launched a military campaign that forced the Viet Minh into the northern part of the country.

Hoping for American support, Ho Chi Minh wrote to President Harry Truman. But the United States refused to help a Communist. During the period known as the cold war, the United States and Communist countries like the Soviet Union feared and distrusted each other. Some people even believed that Communists wanted to take over the U.S. government. The world had seen Communists defeat other nations in Eastern Europe. Those who opposed such takeovers were treated brutally. When Communists gained power in a country, there was no more private property. Everything belonged to the government. Freedom of speech and freedom of religion were suppressed.

Instead of responding to Ho Chi Minh's plea, the United States supported France in its efforts to regain control of Vietnam. But despite American help, the French suffered terrible losses. French citizens were sick of the fighting. They pressured their government into accepting a peace agreement at the Geneva Conference in Switzerland. According to the settlement, Vietnam would be temporarily divided into two sections at the 17th parallel (a geographic line running east-west). French soldiers would occupy the southern part of the country until they could safely return home. Viet Minh troops were to withdraw to the North. Elections were scheduled for July 1956. After the elections, Vietnam would be united as an independent nation.

Ngo Dinh Diem

From the beginning, the United States was worried about this arrangement. Ho Chi Minh was a popular leader. If he were chosen to head the new government, Vietnam would become a Communist country. In contrast, the prime minister of South Vietnam, Ngo Dinh Diem, was a strong anti-Communist. The United States never signed the Geneva Accords, and neither did Ngo Dinh Diem. In October of 1955, Diem held elections in South Vietnam only.

Diem had agents stationed at every polling place. Although he won by a landslide, the results were almost certainly rigged. In Saigon and several other places, the number of votes cast for Diem surpassed the total number of people registered to vote.[1] After he was elected, Diem condemned the elections called for by the Geneva agreement, which would unite North and South Vietnam. He said that such elections could not be "absolutely free."[2]

Even in South Vietnam, many people opposed Diem's policies. In his efforts to defeat the Viet Minh, Diem had his soldiers force villagers to leave their homes, sometimes at gunpoint. They were taken to special settlements where they would not come under Communist influence. Diem drafted young men into the army. And he undid the land reforms that had been put into effect by the Viet Minh. His soldiers took land away from the peasants and gave it back to its former owners.

For a while, the United States supported Diem with military advisers and funds. Finally, even the American officials could no longer tolerate his policies. When Diem died in a military uprising in November 1963, the situation grew worse. The government was in chaos, while the Communists continued to gain followers.

The Unpopular War

Less than a month after Diem's death, President John Kennedy was assassinated. The new president, Lyndon Johnson, decided to take a hard stand against communism in Vietnam. He felt it was up to the United States to preserve freedom in Southeast Asia. If Vietnam fell to the Communists, another country might topple, then another, until all of Southeast Asia was Communist. This idea was known as the domino theory. Johnson would not risk weakening the influence the United States had in Asia or in other parts of the world. Under his administration, the United States launched secret raids against railroads and bridges in the Communist North.

American ships hovered close to North Vietnam. On August 2, 1964, the USS _Maddox_ was reportedly attacked by Communist gunboats. Immediately, more ships were ordered to the Gulf of Tonkin, where the skirmish had taken place. Reports reached the United States that shots were fired against both the *Maddox* and the USS *Turner Joy* on the night of August 4. The two destroyers returned fire, but afterward Chief Officer John J. Herrick began to question what had really happened. It had been too dark to see the enemy, and the radar on the *Maddox* had been reacting strangely. What had seemed at first to be enemy boats might have been simply rain or high waves or even mechanical interference. Herrick said that "the entire action leaves many doubts" and that no one made "actual visual sightings" of the enemy.[3]

Few people, however, knew of Herrick's qualms, and President Johnson did not wait for an investigation. Immediately, Congress passed the Gulf of Tonkin Resolution. President Johnson was authorized to "take all necessary measures to repel any armed attack against forces of the United States and to prevent further aggression."[4] This meant that the president would not have to wait for congressional approval if he felt he needed to act at once.

A Nation Divided

The president wished to reassure Americans. "We seek no wider war," he declared. But he had a warning too. "Whether or not this course can be

A demonstrator offers a flower to a military policeman in Arlington, Virginia, in 1967. Many Americans opposed the war in Vietnam and showed their beliefs through peaceful protest.

maintained lies with the North Vietnamese," he said.[5] However, the Communists continued to attack U.S. sites in Vietnam. Using the broad power Congress had given him, the president decided to send land forces to protect military installations. By the end of March 1965, five thousand Marines had landed in Vietnam.[6] More followed swiftly. In July, President Johnson said that he was increasing the rate at which young men would be drafted into the military. He wanted 175,000 marines and soldiers in Vietnam by the end of the year. [7]

Those who wanted the United States to engage in all-out war were called "hawks." They believed that military might was the way to keep America strong and to overcome the Viet Minh in the North—and also those in South Vietnam who supported communism. (Sometimes this latter group was called the Vietcong). If the United States presented a strong enough show of force, both these groups would be forced into submission. The spread of communism would be stopped.

People who opposed the war in Vietnam were known as "doves." They did not believe it was America's place to defeat communism everywhere in the world. Vietnam was no threat to national security, they said, but young American servicemen were dying. The doves wanted Vietnam left alone to settle its own affairs. They scheduled a peace march in Washington, D.C., for April 17, 1965. About two thousand people were expected. Instead, twenty-five thousand showed up. Seven months later, in the middle of October, the National Coordinating Committee to End the War in Vietnam held protests all over the country. During the demonstrations, many young men burned their draft cards, even though this was illegal.[8] They were telling the president and the whole nation that they would not fight a war that they believed to be wrong.

This was also the message of the protest on November 28, 1965, in which John and Christopher marched. A sociologist summed up the feelings of many in the crowd when he called the war "cruelly immoral and politically stupid."[9] His words drew a loud round of applause.

John, Christopher, and Mary Beth wanted everyone to know where they stood on the war. Wearing a black armband seemed a very mild protest compared to the public burning of draft cards. The students believed the school board was infringing on their liberty. They were determined to establish their right to free speech.

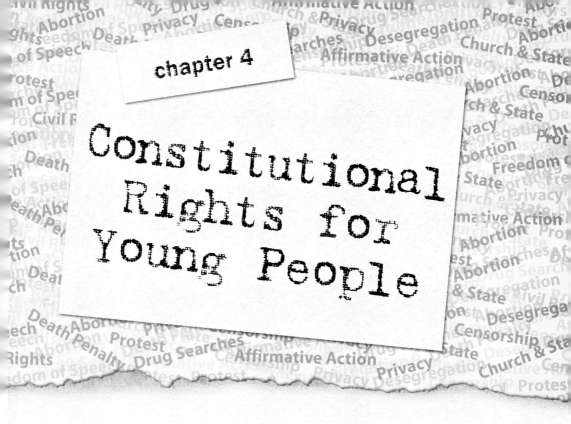

chapter 4

Constitutional Rights for Young People

Once the school administrators announced the ban on black armbands, they expected to be obeyed without question. The very idea of free speech for students was novel. Schools were not democracies, and students did not have a vote on how they should be run. Principals controlled the schools and believed they knew what was best for all the students.

Traditionally, teachers also wielded a great deal of power. In the past, they had been allowed to punish students for very small offenses, as one 1887 court case reveals. A ten-year-old girl had walked to school in temperatures eighteen degrees below zero. When she finally arrived, she was sent home for being tardy. Trudging home through the bitter weather, the child suffered frostbite. Her indignant parents filed a lawsuit against the school. However, the court ruled that the school had the right to make and enforce its own rules. The parents' case was dismissed.[1]

Although this case sounds shocking, in the 1880s few people would take a child's side over the school system. In or out of the classroom, children had little in the way of legal rights. Their parents or guardians were allowed to treat them almost as property.[2] Often children were forced to go to work at a very early age. Many had little chance to attend school or to play. The law did not give them the right to their own salaries. Parents could use the money their children made in any way they saw fit. In many cases, families depended on their children's income in order to survive.

New Rights for Students

By the beginning of the twentieth century, however, reformers realized that children deserved certain basic rights. They should not have the same responsibilities as adults. Children needed the freedom to grow and develop and learn. The reformers began working for laws to establish and safeguard these rights for children. Three important gains were made: (1) New laws required that all children attend school. (2) Child labor was greatly restricted. No longer could children work at exhausting jobs for eight to ten hours a day or even longer. (3) A separate court system was created for children who broke the law. When children got into trouble, they would no longer be tried as if they were adults, nor would they be put in jail with hardened criminals.[3]

"Children Should Be Seen and Not Heard"

Although these reforms protected children, the new measures did not give them the same rights that adults had. The first ten amendments to the Constitution, which are known as the Bill of Rights, spell out exactly what freedoms are guaranteed to American citizens. These include freedom of religion and freedom of speech. No one suggested that children choose what church or synagogue they attended. That was up to their parents to decide for them. Parents could also instruct their children to keep silent at certain times or limit them to certain topics. The old saying "Children should be seen and not heard" still summed up the feelings of many people.

In school, students certainly didn't have the right to say whatever they wished. Learning to be good citizens meant conforming to certain generally accepted values. Schools taught these values, and children were not supposed to question them. Obeying rules—not challenging

Until the early twentieth century, children could be forced to work at exhausting full-time jobs. This little girl was photographed in a North Carolina mill in 1908.

them—was considered an important part of all students' education. A judge from Maine expressed the prevailing view:

> Free political institutions are only possible where the great body of the people are moral, intelligent, and habituated [used] to self-control, and to obedience to lawful authority. . . . To become good citizens, children must be taught self-restraint, obedience, and other civil virtues.[4]

Critical thought and self-expression had no place in the judge's list. A good student was quiet, mannerly, and did exactly what he or she was told.

West Virginia v. Barnett

How far did the obedience requirement extend? Might there be any circumstances in which a student had the constitutional right to disobey a school regulation? A 1943 case, *West Virginia Board of Education* v. *Barnett*, concerned the rights of students who did not want to pledge allegiance to the flag. Several students who were Jehovah's Witnesses claimed that the pledge went against their religious beliefs.

School officials did not accept their objections. The United States was in the midst of World War II, and the pledge was considered a way to show patriotism. Finally, the principal expelled the students who refused to salute the flag. The students, however, felt that officials had a duty to respect their religion. They decided to take their case to court.

Siding with the students, the court declared that in forcing students to say the pledge, the school had exceeded its authority. The court also championed freedom of expression and belief:

> If there is any fixed star in our constitutional constellation, it is that no official, high or petty, can prescribe what shall be orthodox [accepted] in politics, nationalism, religion, or other matters of opinion or force citizens to confess by word or act their faith therein. If there are any circumstances which permit an exception, they do not now occur to us.[5]

Although this ruling did not guarantee free speech for students, it did uphold their rights to have their own beliefs. Schools could not force them to act against those beliefs.

Students Become Vocal

Throughout the 1950s and early 1960s, order and respect for authority reigned in the classroom. But as casualties mounted on both sides of the war in Vietnam, many young people began to question what they were being told by the government. Was it really necessary for the United States to intervene in Vietnam? Did the government have the right to order young men to fight? Was this a just war? To many Americans, young and old, human life was more precious than any political ideal. Many students could not remain silent—even when they had to break school rules to speak out.

Antiwar demonstrations made headlines on college campuses all over the nation. When military recruiters visited campuses, the situation became especially heated. Sometimes the protesters tried to prevent interested students from talking to the recruiters. Before 1967, there was no precedent for constitutional rights for those who had not reached the legal age for adulthood. But angry students weren't concerned with what the courts said. They claimed their right of free speech anyway. "Hell, no, we won't go!" became the rallying cry of young men who opposed the war.

As students found their voices, they started making other demands. They wanted more classes that related to their interests and to what was happening in the real world. African Americans, fighting for their civil rights, wanted courses in black history. Courses in women's history were also in demand. On some college campuses, students questioned graduation requirements. Before this, it was always school administrators who set the curriculum. In some ways, the educational establishment of an earlier era had been turned upside down.

Disillusionment with the war spilled over into other areas. A counterculture sprang up known as the "hippie" movement. Hippies wanted to stress their differences from the rest of society. They chose lifestyles and music and clothing that set them apart. They refused to do what was expected of them, and they favored artistic expression over competitive careers. They certainly were not afraid to challenge adults in authority.

The *Gault* Case

As college administrators were dealing with student demonstrations, a small court case was unfolding in Gila County, Arizona. Although it had nothing to do with protests, it was to send a big message in terms of young people's rights. A fifteen-year-old named Gerald Francis Gault had been arrested for making an obscene phone call. Although Gerald denied making the call, he did admit to doing the dialing. According to Gerald, his friend did the actual talking.

Gerald's parents were at work when he was taken into custody. When Mr. and Mrs. Gault arrived home, they had no idea where their son was. They had to discover what happened from the family of Gerald's friend, who had also been taken into custody. Gerald's family was informed of the date of his hearing, but the exact charges against him were not specified.

During the proceedings, the judge ignored many rights required by law for adult offenders. Gerald was not represented by a lawyer. He did not have a chance to confront Mrs. Cook, the woman who made the charges against him. Gerald's mother had asked that Mrs. Cook attend, but the judge said that "she didn't have to be present at that hearing."[6]

In further violation of usual safeguards, no transcript was made of Gerald's hearing. When the proceedings were over, the judge sentenced Gerald to the State Industrial School, a facility for juvenile delinquents, until he was twenty-one.

Not surprisingly, the Gault family sought to have the case reviewed. Without a transcript of the hearing, however, they faced an uphill battle. Eventually, the Gaults took the case all the way to the Supreme Court.

In 1967, the Supreme Court reversed the judgment of the lower court and said that constitutional guarantees traditionally reserved for adults in the court system also applied to children. Writing the majority opinion, Justice Abe Fortas conceded that most juvenile court jurisdictions did not grant the same rights as adults received when facing trial. But after reviewing the purpose of the juvenile justice system, the justice declared:

> Under our Constitution, the condition of being a boy does not justify a kangaroo court. . . . The essential difference between Gerald's case and a normal criminal case is that safeguards available to adults were discarded in Gerald's case. The summary procedure as well as the long commitment was possible because Gerald was 15 years of age instead of over eighteen. . . ."[7]

The *Gault* case had established legal protection for minors. These included the right to be represented by a lawyer, the right to face their accusers, and the right not to testify against themselves. In effect, the Court was saying that the Constitution was for children as well as for adults. This was a big victory for students.[8]

When the _Gault_ decision was handed down, _Tinker_ v. Des _Moines_ was still making its way through the courts. Young people as well as those over eighteen believed that they had a right to protest what was happening in Vietnam. John, Christopher, and Mary Beth were determined to see children's First Amendment right to free speech acknowledged by the courts.

chapter 5

Taking a Stand for Free Speech

The Eckhardts, the Tinkers, and other families who believed in the right to protest had no time to waste. On January 3, 1966, the school board had upheld the principals' rule against wearing armbands. The same night many of the interested families gathered at the Eckhardt house. Two lawyers from the Iowa Civil Liberties Union (ICLU) joined them. Although the school board vote had gone against the protesters, the lawyers were impressed with what the students had accomplished, even calling it "a miracle."[1] The students had not proved their case to the school board, but they had done something even more important. They had brought the issue before the public. According to the lawyers, the students had stimulated record numbers of people to think about civil liberties. Des Moines newspapers had been flooded with articles. *The New York Times* and the CBS evening news had also covered the story.

John, Mary Beth, Christopher, and some other students would have liked to keep on wearing arm-bands—even if it meant missing school. But the lawyers advised against it. If the students continued to disobey the school board, it might lessen public sympathy for their cause. In addition, the lawyers didn't want any question of truancy to cloud the issues in a court case. There was another way the students could express mourning for the casualties in Vietnam. They could simply wear black clothing.

A great deal of discussion followed the lawyers' suggestion. "Some thought it was accepting defeat to return [to school] without the armbands," John recalled. "Others said this would clear the decks for a legal case."[2] Already the lawyers felt certain that a strong case could be made supporting the students' free speech rights.

Meanwhile, the armband controversy had caught the attention of William Kunstler, a well-known lawyer with a reputation for defending unpopular positions. Kunstler called Lorena Jeanne Tinker from New York. He offered to represent her children and Christopher Eckhardt pro bono (without charge). "I think it's going to be a landmark case," he said.[3]

However, the ICLU thought it would be best if its own lawyers handled the case. There would be no problem with funding. Louise Noun, the chairperson of the ICLU, donated a large sum of money to support the armband case. "Our family didn't have a great deal of money," Mary Beth recalled years later. "We couldn't have pursued a lawsuit on our own. When I found out we were going to court, I was happy that the school board's ruling was not going to be the end."[4]

Back to School

The day after the school board meeting, the protesters returned to school dressed in black. "We went back to school," explained Christopher years later, "not because we believed the school board was right, but because the school board had the might."[5] With their position highly publicized, the Eckhardts received a great deal of hate mail—even after Christopher's father took a job in Canada in 1967.[6]

As the year progressed, Christopher and other students gradually added colors to their attire. But John wore black the rest of the school year. "I kind of stood out," he recalls.[7] Supportive teachers invited him to speak with their classes about his beliefs. Although some classmates encouraged him, others called him "a traitor, a coward, and a Commie."[8] One day, in the school swimming pool, a boy held John underwater and condemned his views on the war. And on Memorial Day, John was not permitted to march with the rest of the school band in the parade. Overall, however, he says that the pending lawsuit "didn't affect me as much as you might think."[9] He went to classes, hung out with friends, and defended his views when called upon.

On March 14, 1966, Dan Johnston, a lawyer with the ICLU, filed an official complaint with the Iowa district court. Although a number of students had been suspended, only the Tinker children, Christopher Eckhardt, and their fathers were listed in the lawsuit. According to some speculation, fear of repercussions in the workplace may have influenced some families not to join the suit.[10] Bruce Clark disagrees. He believes that some families simply were not interested or had other priorities. Bruce himself felt no interest in joining the lawsuit. He was scheduled to graduate in a few months. "At that point, the war had become more important to me than whether I could wear an armband," he recalled.[11]

Johnston named twenty-three defendants in the *Tinker* v. *Des Moines* lawsuit. These included Ora Niffenegger and other members of the school board as well as school Superintendent Dwight Davis and some principals and teachers.

The students (known as the plaintiffs) made two demands of the school officials (known as the defendants). They wanted the right to wear armbands to express their feeling about the war. They also wanted the school district to cover any legal expenses and to pay them one dollar in damages. The reason for the dollar fee was simple. Dan Johnston knew that the case could take a long time winding through the courts. John and Christopher might graduate before it was settled. Or the students might decide they no longer cared about armbands. If this occurred, the case could be declared "moot"—no longer relevant—and no final decision would be issued. The larger issue of free speech rights for students would not be solved. When money is at stake, however, even a very small amount, a case cannot be declared moot. By asking for a dollar, Johnston made sure that the case would be kept alive, no matter what the plaintiffs were doing. The issue of free speech would have to be addressed.

"I Morally Think It's Wrong"

On July 25, 1966, *Tinker* v. *Des Moines* came to trial. That same day a headline in the *Des Moines Register* read: "A Lot of Dead Marines."[12] The United States had lost three hundred aircraft during the past six months. In a single week in July, 737 ground soldiers died.[13] The right to

***amicus curiae* (plural, *amici curiae*)**—Literally, "friend of the court"; someone who files a brief in a case in which that person is not a party but has a strong interest. Such briefs let the court benefit from the added viewpoint.

appellant or petitioner—The person who thinks the lower court made an error.

appellate court (sometimes called a court of appeals)—A court that reviews decisions of lower courts for fairness and accuracy. An appellate court can reverse the ruling of a lower court.

appellee or respondent—The person who won the case in the lower court.

brief—Written statement of a party's argument on one or more issues in the case.

concur—To agree with the ruling in a court case.

dissent—To disagree with the ruling in a court case.

majority opinion—The ruling and reasoning supported by a majority of appellate court judges in a case. **Concurring opinions** are written by judges who agree with the majority holding but have other reasons for their views. **Dissenting opinions** are written by judges who disagree with the ruling of the majority.

precedent—A legal holding that will determine how courts decide future cases.

writ of certiorari—An order granted by the United States Supreme Court when a party applies to the Court to review the decision of a lower court and the Supreme Court agrees to do so.

mourn these deaths and to protest the war was more important to the plaintiffs than ever.

John Tinker was the first plaintiff to take the stand. Philip Lovrien, one of the school district's lawyers, tried to show that someone else had persuaded John to wear the armband. He wanted to know who it was. John resisted this implication strongly. No one had convinced him. Wearing the armband was his own personal decision. John emphasized the position when his own attorney, Dan Johnston, questioned him on reexamination. "It was my own view," he declared, "I like to think I thought it out myself."[14]

To stress his point still further, John explained that his father had initially been hesitant about the armbands. Then John told his father that he considered the armband "a matter of conscience."[15] The strength of John's convictions had changed Leonard Tinker's mind. Explaining his feelings about war, John declared, "I morally think it's wrong, and when people are getting killed, I guess that's important to me."[16] When Mary Beth and Christopher took the stand, they echoed John's statements. No one had forced or even encouraged them to wear armbands. They had freely chosen this way to express their feelings about the war.

A total of ten witnesses testified, including seven from the school district. Ora Niffenegger recalled his words to Bruce Clark and Ross

Peterson when they phoned him in December. He had explained that the war "should be handled at the ballot box and not in the halls of our public schools."[17]

Ruling in District Court

The plaintiffs and defendants had agreed on a nonjury trial. Judge Roy Stephenson considered the case for five weeks before issuing his decision on September 1, 1966. He ruled in favor of the school district. The ban on armbands would stay in effect. According to the judge, administrators had a "reasonable basis" for what they had done. "In this instance . . ." declared the judge, "it is the disciplined atmosphere of the classroom, not the plaintiffs' right to wear armbands on school premises, which is entitled to the protection of the law."[18]

Despite the defeat, the students had something to be happy about. The judge stated that he accepted the reason for their protest. It meant a great deal to John, Christopher, and Mary Beth that he understood their motives—mourning the casualties and supporting the Christmas truce.[19] Although the students were disappointed, their lawyer, Dan Johnston, was not surprised by the outcome of the trial.[20] From the start, he had realized that the plaintiffs faced an uphill battle. But he also thought the students had excellent grounds to

Lorena Jeanne Tinker, Mary Beth's mother, sits with her at a school board meeting. The three students' parents supported their opposition to the war.

appeal the decision. "It was a foregone conclusion that we would go on," remembered John Tinker.[21]

Appealing the Decision

The plaintiffs had several reasons for hoping their appeal would be successful. Judge Stephenson's ruling conflicted with a recent decision of the Fifth Circuit Court of Appeals. In *Burnside* v. *Byars*, the court upheld the right of students at a Mississippi school to wear "freedom buttons," supporting the civil rights movement, provided the buttons did not disrupt class. A similar case, *Blackwell* v. *Issaquena County Board of Education*, had been decided differently because the buttons the students wore had caused major disturbances in the school. Some people concluded that since the black armbands had not led to classroom interruption or violence, the *Burnside* standard should apply to the *Tinker* case as well.

Johnston was also hopeful because of another fact he had been able to establish at the district trial. Although Des Moines school officials had suspended students for wearing armbands, they had allowed other students to wear campaign buttons and religious medals. They had also allowed students to wear black armbands to mourn the death of school spirit. This seemed like a contradiction that the appeals court would have to address.

But a three-member panel of the Court of Appeals was not able to reach a verdict. An unusual step would have to be taken. The case would be heard again en banc. This meant that all the judges of the Eighth Circuit would listen to the arguments and take part in the deliberations.

On November 3, 1967, the justices announced that they were unable to break the stalemate. They had been split 4–4 in their opinions. When an appeals court is equally divided, the decision of the lower court is upheld. That meant the school district was allowed to continue its prohibition of black armbands.

Despite their disappointment, the plaintiffs felt heartened.[22] If they hadn't won, they hadn't really lost either. By this time, John and Christopher were seniors in high school. Mary Beth was a sophomore. There was only one step left to take.

"I knew at the time that the U.S. Supreme Court consisted of nine dudes in black robes who made decisions that affected the rest of the country," Christopher recalled thirty years later. " . . . Never in my wildest dreams did I ever think we would end up in front of the Supreme Court."[23]

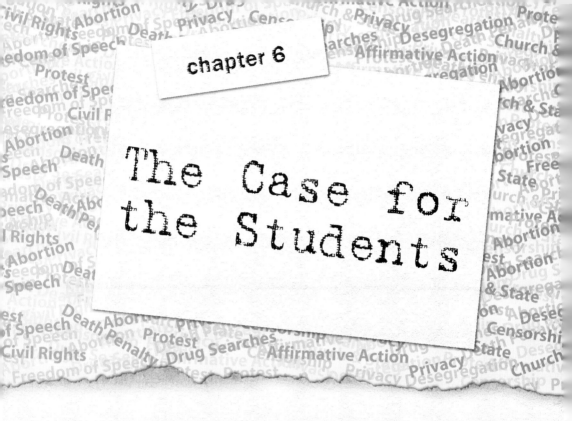

chapter 6

The Case for the Students

The Supreme Court agrees to hear only a small percentage of the cases brought to its attention. Those who wish to bring a case before the Court are called appellants and must file for a writ of certiorari (ser-she-o-rar-ee). They can also be called petitioners because they are petitioning the court to reverse the lower court ruling. The appellants' lawyers must submit a brief showing that the lower court made a mistake. They must also show the relevance of the case to the entire country and the need for a Supreme Court ruling to clarify the issue. The brief becomes the appellants' application for a writ of certiorari. If certiorari is granted, the Supreme Court will hear and rule on a case.

Before composing its brief, the ICLU, which still represented the students, consulted with the national office of the American Civil Liberties Union (ACLU). Although Johnston was still the students' attorney, most of the brief was written by ACLU lawyer David Ellenhorn. ACLU National Legal Director Melvin Wulf also contributed. On January 16, 1968, a brief requesting certiorari in the *Tinker* v. *Des Moines* case was filed. The brief stressed the depth of the students' commitment to peace. It also pointed out that school functioning had not been disturbed by the armbands. In their reply brief, lawyers for the school district claimed there had been some problems.

Protests Multiply

Two years had passed since the armband controversy. Protests against the war continued to multiply. On college campuses, students marched, hoisted antiwar signs, and held rallies. In 1967, Bruce Clark, one of the original organizers of the armband protest, was arrested at the University of Iowa. He had been trying to forcibly escort a recruiter from a chemical company off campus. The recruiter was there to interest students in jobs, but Bruce and some others protested the company's production of chemicals used in Vietnam. A contingent of police on campus added to the tension of the scene. "We didn't let it stop us," Bruce said of his arrest. "We built huge dissent rallies."[1] The vehemence of such demonstrations across the nation made the armband protest look tame by comparison. The issue of student protest loomed large in the national consciousness.

Meanwhile, John, Christopher, and Mary Beth waited for a reply to their brief. Would the Supreme Court decide to hear the case? On March 4, they had their answer. The Supreme Court granted certiorari and scheduled the case to be heard in the fall of 1968. The *Des Moines Register* applauded the Court's acceptance of the case. "School administrators increasingly con-fronted by politically active and militant student bodies will be grateful for any guidance the Supreme Court can give," read one editorial.[2]

The First Amendment

Before they argued their positions before the Supreme Court, both the petitioners and the re-spondents had to submit new briefs. According to Dan Johnston and the other lawyers for the students, freedom of speech encompasses much more than verbal communication. The students might have chosen to discuss their views while walking to class with friends. School officials could not have found anything wrong with that. By wearing armbands, however, John, Christopher, and Mary Beth were doing basically the same thing. They were exercising their right of symbolic free speech. The armbands sent a strong but silent message: We mourn the casualties in Vietnam, and we support a truce.

Dan Johnston thought that John, Christopher, and Mary Beth had a solid argument based on the First Amendment to the Constitution, which reads:

> Congress shall make no law respecting an establishment of religion, or prohibiting the free exercise thereof; or abridging the freedom of speech, or of the press; or the right of the people to peaceably assembly, and to petition the Government for a redress of grievances.

The First Amendment guarantees freedom of speech to all citizens of the United States, argued the appellants, and students are no exception. In addition, the students had rights under the Fourteenth Amendment, which grants all Americans "equal protection of the laws." But instead of being protected, the students' rights were violated without sufficient reason, said the appellants.

Although the attorneys acknowledged that school authorities must maintain order, they also asserted that the Constitution limits what teachers and principals can do. Rights that are valued for adults in a democracy, they argued, should also be encouraged in the schools. To press their point, they quoted from the recent *Gault* case: ". . . the 'Bill of Rights' is not for adults alone."[3]

Past rulings, like the *Gault* case, play a very important role in cases that are brought before the Supreme Court. They establish precedent—or historical support—for a particular outcome. By showing that their position agreed with previous court decisions, the appellants' lawyers further strengthened their case. Another precedent they considered was *West Virginia* v. *Barnette,* which upheld the rights of students not to salute the flag. According to the appellants' lawyers, this decision

> recognized that the protections of the First Amendment are fully applicable to public school students, and that their First Amendment rights cannot be infringed [lessened] even for so lofty a purpose as the promotion of national unity in a time of war.[4]

The lawyers further stated:

> Barnette involved the power of the State to compel students to take part in a patriotic ceremony to which they were conscientiously opposed. The instant case [*Tinker* v. *Des Moines*] involves the power of the State to prohibit students from expressing their views in school. The guiding principle is the same—the State does not have the power to impose uniformity of thought, action and belief among its students by suppressing expressions of dissent.[5]

These members of the Supreme Court heard the case of Tinker v. Des Moines. *Chief Justice Earl Warren is seated center front.*

The students' position gained support from another precedent quoted by the lawyers, *Keyishian* v. *Board of Regents:*

> Our nation is deeply committed to safeguarding academic freedom. . . . That freedom is therefore a special concern of the First Amendment, which does not tolerate laws that cast a pall of orthodoxy [sameness] over the classroom. The vigilant protection of constitutional freedom is nowhere more vital than in the community of American schools.[6]

This means that all sides of current events and political issues must be taught and discussed in schools. There is no single proper or correct view that can be imposed. It is as valid to criticize United States foreign policy as it is to support it. The whole concept of democracy depends on the free exchange of ideas. Students need to be exposed to many different positions so that they can make up their own minds about issues. If free speech is to be meaningful in American society, students must learn it while they are young. It is not enough for them to merely memorize the words of the First Amendment. They must practice the right of free speech themselves.

An Orderly Protest

School officials feared that arguments, physical fights, perhaps even rioting might result from the armband protest. However, nothing of the sort occurred. The appellants contended that the black armbands were a "dignified, orderly, and peaceful" way for the students to convey their feelings about the Vietnam War.[7] There was no threat to the educational routine or the rights of any other students. John, Christopher, and Mary Beth did not want to disrupt normal school activities. The sole purpose of the protest was to stimulate calm and thoughtful discussion. Their moral and religious beliefs played a large role in their decision to wear the armbands.

In view of all this, were school officials justified in expecting serious problems as a result of the armbands? According to Johnston's brief:

> [School officials] had no reason to believe [the] petitioners would wear the arm bands in such a manner as to deliberately provoke a disturbance or a breach of discipline. Nor does the record show any basis for a judgment that the arm bands could not have been worn by petitioners without inevitably causing a disturbance. Apparently, then, the principals held the mistaken view that they had the power to ban free speech by students arbitrarily and completely.[8]

If Violence Occurs

Even if administrators had good reason to suspect serious disruptions, that in itself would not be enough to outlaw the protest, the appellants' attorneys argued. If school principals had observed serious problems, they should not hold the protesters at fault. The appellants were simply expressing their views in a peaceful way. The students who reacted with hostility to the armbands should be held responsible. Instead of becoming violent, they could choose to exercise their own free speech in a proper manner. It is not fair to take away the free speech of one group of students (those who oppose the war) because another group of students (those who support the war) cannot control themselves. The individuals who did the shouting, pushing, or fighting are the ones who should be punished.

Double Standard

According to their legal team, John, Christopher, and Mary Beth were not suspended for behaving in a disruptive manner. They were suspended for disobeying a rule "specifically designed to impede [them] in the exercise of their First Amendment rights."[9] But not everyone's rights were violated. The prohibition against black armbands discriminated against those who held a particular viewpoint. Some manifestations of symbolic speech were tolerated. Students could wear campaign buttons for presidential elections. Some students had even worn an Iron Cross, a symbol that had been formerly associated with the Nazi party. Religious medals were also allowed.

The brief asked, Why should some students be permitted to express their beliefs symbolically when others were not? It represented a double standard. A viewpoint that school officials believed to be unpopular was suppressed. According to the petitioners' brief, the ban on armbands struck at the very heart of the First Amendment—"the expression of views which may be unpalatable [unacceptable] to predominant public sentiment."[10] Protecting such views is what the First Amendment is all about, the lawyers said.

Amicus Curiae

In addition to the attorneys for both sides, a party interested in the outcome of a Supreme Court case is also permitted to file a brief as a "friend of the court." This is known as an *amicus curiae* brief. An organization called the National School Association (NSA), which included representatives of many college student governments, decided to do this. Members of the NSA felt they had a strong stake in the outcome of the *Tinker* case because it would affect protests on college campuses all over the country. In its brief, the NSA claimed that the armbands worn by John, Christopher, and Mary Beth did not pose a "clear and present" danger to the school system.[11] Because of this, the principals had no right to restrict the students' free speech, the brief stated.

The appellants and their lawyers as well as the NSA clearly believed that the school district's actions were unconstitutional. But school officials did not see the issue as one of free speech. They felt that their right to run effective schools for the good of all the students was at stake. In their reply brief, they tried to disprove the petitioners' arguments.

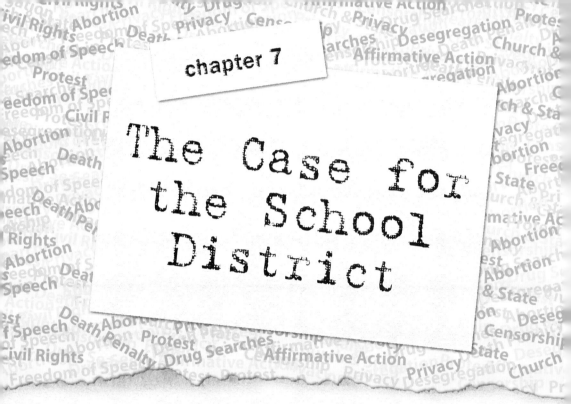

chapter 7

The Case for the School District

Allan Herrick, the attorney who took the lead in preparing the brief for the appellees, also called the respondents, believed firmly in law and order. A veteran of World War I, he supported U.S. foreign policy. Despite the testimony of the Tinkers and Christopher Eckhardt, he did not believe the decision to wear armbands had been theirs alone. He suspected that some radical organization, such as Students for a Democratic Society (SDS) had influenced them. He also thought that their parents might have encouraged their protest.[1] This bothered Herrick a great deal. Herrick believed that "parents should tell their children . . . to obey the rules and not to rock the boat in school."[2] They should not interfere with the efforts of school administrators to do their jobs. Neither should the courts.

The Greater Good

According to the school district's lawyers, the Constitution does not guarantee freedom of speech in all circumstances. Sometimes rules or laws made in the best interest of the majority of people limits free speech in certain situations. Such rules are permitted as long as they are "not intended to control the content of speech."[3] School officials claimed that they were not trying to suppress criticism of the United States' role in Vietnam. They were simply trying to maintain order for the greater good of the school.

To bolster the idea of limited free speech, Herrick quoted the 1966 case of *Blackwell* v. *Issaquena County Board of Education*. "The constitutional guarantee of freedom of speech 'does not confer an absolute right to speak' and the law recognizes that there can be an abuse of such freedom."[4] The appellees contended that an abuse had taken place in the armband case. They claimed that the protest had been planned by the SDS and supported by the Women's International League for Peace and Freedom, another organization that was highly critical of the Vietnam War. Four Tinker children—John, Mary Beth, Hope, and Paul—had worn armbands to school with their parents' blessing. Herrick posed the question:

> Is it more reasonable to conclude that [the children] were doing this as matter of conscience in the exercise of their constitutional rights, or is Reverend Tinker, the secretary for Peace and Education [a Quaker organization], through his children, undertaking to infiltrate the school with his propaganda?[5]

The brief implied that the second alternative was by far the more likely. Using his children to spread his own views was something that Leonard Tinker had no right to do.

The schools had a lot to lose if confusion and hostility replaced an orderly environment. But, according to the appellees' brief, the students would not lose very much by obeying the rule not to wear armbands. After all, they could put them on to go to the store, to church, to ride their bicycles. In fact, they could wear black armbands anywhere in the community outside of school. While they were on campus, they could talk about their views. There was no school rule against sharing their ideas with friends and classmates in quiet discussion. The students were not completely losing their freedom of speech.

Reasons for the Ban

School officials felt that they had excellent reasons for outlawing black armbands. A young man from a local high school had recently been killed in Vietnam. Some students might feel that a protest against the war dishonored his memory. Others might view his death as a tragic reminder that the war had to stop. If students started to demonstrate, school authorities believed they would have a hard time containing the situation.

A second reason why officials felt justified in banning armbands had to do with their purpose. Mary Beth, John, Christopher, and other students said they wore armbands as a way of mourning the dead. However, the school had other means to do this. Special assemblies were held on Veterans' Day and Memorial Day. These cere-monies honored the dead without posing the risk of class disruptions.

In advancing the school district's case, the appellees' brief listed several more arguments favoring the ban on armbands. One concerned the mandatory nature of school. All students between the ages of six and sixteen were required to attend classes. Basically, they were a "captive audience."[6] Perhaps they had no desire to witness an antiwar protest and the possible resulting disturbance. If the event took place anywhere else, they could sim-ply leave. At school, however, there was no place they could escape. Students were forced to see the protesters' views paraded before them. To school officials, this seemed an infringement of the rights of students who opposed the protest.

What Is a Disruption?

Lawyers for John, Mary Beth, and Christopher said that their armbands had not caused any disturbance. In its brief, however, the school district said that the normal school day _had_ been disrupted. Seeing the armbands distracted some students from their purpose in coming to school. Several students had made taunting remarks to John. Mary Beth had received some unfriendly comments. There was also evidence that someone had struck either Ross Peterson or Bruce Clark. If the school principals hadn't decided to ban armbands, there could have been more angry confrontations and even violence.[7] Students might have been hurt. School officials did not think they had to wait until someone was injured to take action. They should be able to make rules to prevent anyone from being hurt in the first place.

The problems that occurred in the schools might seem small. But school officials' lawyers pointed out that different standards should be used to judge disruptions in different places. Someone yelling his views outside—perhaps in the park or maybe on the street—is not the same as someone yelling his views inside a school building. The first situation may not attract much notice, but the second situation is certain to attract lots of attention.[8] The appellees looked to an earlier court case, *Brown* v. *Louisiana,* to make their point: "Disturbances in Schools Are Not Properly Measured by Identical Standards Used to Measure Disturbances on the Street, in Eating Houses or Bus Depots."[9] Principals and teachers should have the right to decide if and when a school day is disrupted.

Who's Running the Schools?

In prohibiting armbands, the Des Moines principals did not violate any state or federal law. Their action did not contradict a previous ruling of the Supreme Court. Justices on the Court might not think that the armband regulation was necessary or wise. But they were not there to judge the rule. They were there to judge whether or not school officials had abused their authority in making the rule. The appellees stoutly maintained that they had not. They made the point forcefully in their brief:

> The law in Iowa and elsewhere gives school authorities the right to adopt reasonable rules and regulations governing the conduct of the pupils. If the regulation is reasonable in the light of existing facts and circumstances the court may not question the discretion [wisdom] vested in the school authorities. It is not for the courts to

consider whether the rule in retrospect was wise or expedient [practical or necessary] so long as it was a reasonable exercise of the discretion vested in the school authorities.[10]

Simply put, the brief said that school authorities in Des Moines had been doing their job to the best of their ability. The courts had no right to interfere. The right of a few students to express themselves did not outweigh the right of the principals to safeguard the schools for everyone. The ban on armbands had slightly limited but had not seriously harmed free speech. It was necessary to ensure safety and a proper learning environment.

On to the Supreme Court

Both sides had presented their case on paper. Soon it would be time for the lawyers to make their arguments in person before the Supreme Court. John and Christopher had already graduated from high school. They would no longer benefit if the schools were forced to allow armbands. But they cared desperately about the case—as did Mary Beth and countless students across the country. Did they have the constitutional right to protest? Under what circumstances? The response of the Supreme Court to *Tinker* v. *Des Moines* would answer these critical questions.

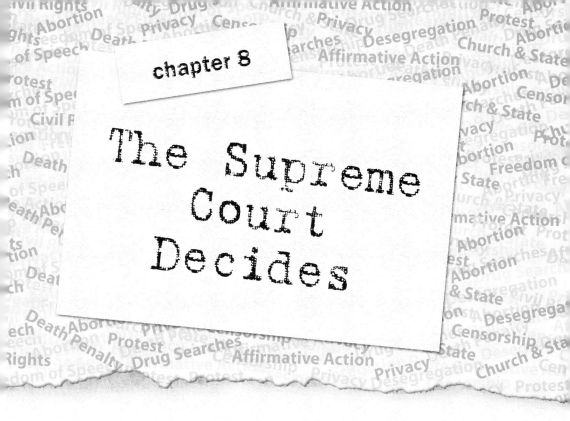

chapter 8

The Supreme Court Decides

John, Christopher, and Mary Beth would not be testifying before the Supreme Court. Appellants and appellees are never heard as witnesses. This is because the Court is not trying to determine what happened. The justices accept the facts of the case. Their role is to decide whether the lower court ruled correctly.

Only the lawyers on each side would be permitted to make a half-hour presentation and to answer questions from the justices. But, of course, the appellants wanted to hear the proceedings. Christopher came to Washington, D.C., for the oral arguments on November 12, 1968. John had also hoped to attend, but he missed his flight. He would have to rely on secondhand reports to learn what was said and how the justices reacted to the lawyers' statements.

Oral Arguments

Speaking for the students, Dan Johnston summarized the issues at stake. He said that there needed to be a

> correct balance between the interest of the school in maintain[ing] discipline and decorum and the rights of the students who . . . are increasingly moved to have opinions and to wish to express those opinions.[1]

Justice Hugo Black wanted to know if the free speech principle would extend even to kindergarten. While acknowledging the difference between a kindergartner's views and the more considered views of an older student, Johnston said that yes, they should have free speech too.

Allan Herrick opened for the school district with a brief summation of what the administrators considered to be the basic issues: (1) Schools should be able to set rules to prevent violence _before_ it occurs. (2) All rules restrict freedom to some extent. Did the court really want to review all of them? (3) Disturbances in the classroom are not the same as disturbances on the street. Different standards apply.[2]

Justice Marshall asked how many students had actually worn armbands. As far as Herrick could tell, there were about seven. This seemed to surprise the justice. "Seven out of eighteen thousand," he repeated with a hint of amazement, "and the school board was afraid that seven students wearing arm-bands would disrupt eighteen thousand."[3]

Thirty years later, Christopher Eckhardt recalled his excitement on hearing the justice's comment. "Then I was confident we would pre-vail," he said.[4] But Christopher, John, and Mary Beth had to wait more than three months for the ruling. As students all over the nation continued to protest the war, Americans were eager hear what the Supreme Court would say.

"Out of the Blue"

None of the appellants were present in the Supreme Court on February 24, 1969. Later that day, however, Christopher and John, freshmen in college, received phone calls from reporters. At first Christopher, who attended Mankato State University in Minnesota, didn't understand what his caller was talking about. Why was he being congratulated? The reporter had to spell it out for Christopher. "You won your Supreme Court case." Then he asked Christopher how he felt about the victory. "I love it!" replied Christopher. "I've been waiting three years to hear it!" He declared himself "overjoyed and overwhelmed."[5]

John, then at the University of Iowa, recalled that his phone call also came "totally out of the blue." He told the reporter that he was "excited" and "glad."[6]

By this time, the Tinkers had moved to Missouri. Mary Beth, a junior in high school, got the good news from her mother when she arrived home. The family held a small celebration with ice cream. Mary Beth's father was sorry he couldn't be home to share the excitement. Leonard Tinker learned of the Supreme Court decision in Paris, France, where he was attending peace meetings.

The Schoolhouse Gate

The Supreme Court, in a 7–2 vote, made it very clear that students had rights. Writing for the majority, Justice Abe Fortas declared, "It can hardly be argued that either students or teachers shed their constitutional rights to freedom of speech or expression at the schoolhouse gate."[7] Although the Court upheld freedom of speech for students, it also recognized the authority of school administrators to regulate behavior and create an orderly learning environment. "Our problem," explained Justice Fortas, "lies in the area where students in the exercise of First Amendment rights collide with the rules of the school authorities."[8]

The Court had weighed all the evidence and concluded that the armband protest had not posed a threat to the effective running of the schools. The concerns of the school officials did not justify their

Justice Abe Fortas wrote the majority opinion in the Tinker *case, saying that students do not "shed their constitutional rights . . . at the schoolhouse gate." Only Justices Black and Harlan dissented.*

quickly formulated rule against armbands. Any time a student expressed an unpopular view, there is always the risk of a heated exchange. "But our Constitution says we must take this risk," concluded Fortas.[9]

Most of the justices felt that the school district had been trying to avoid controversy. But they had no right to eliminate controversial discussions from school. The rule against armbands had targeted a single viewpoint—opposition to the Vietnam War. It was not fair to deny some students the right to protest the war in this nondisruptive manner while allowing other students to wear campaign buttons and even the Iron Cross. The justices considered it significant that armbands had been forbidden only after a student, Ross Peterson, had wanted to publish an article about Vietnam in the school newspaper. Fortas went on to explain:

> In our system, state-operated schools may not be enclaves of totalitarianism [dictatorship]. School officials do not possess absolute authority over their students. Students in school as well as out of school are "persons" under the Constitution. They are possessed of fundamental rights which the State must respect, just as they themselves must respect their obligations to the State.[10]

As long as they didn't cause a commotion that hindered others from learning, students were free to express their views. Schools exist to foster certain kinds of experiences, Justice Fortas explained. One of them is "personal intercommunication among the students."[11] This exchange of ideas is more than just a casual activity. It is a vital part of the students' education and an important preparation for adulthood. During a supervised class discussion, a student has the right to raise his hand and explain his view. This freedom of expression extends to all parts of the school, such as the cafeteria or athletic fields. Fortas put it in simple, strong language: "The Constitution says that Congress (and the States) may not abridge the right to free speech. This provision means what it says."[12]

Dissent

Two justices disagreed with the majority ruling. Siding with the appellees, Justice John Marshall Harlan said that school officials should be given "the widest authority in maintaining discipline and good order."[13]

Justice Hugo Black also had a great deal more to say on the matter. In a bitter dissent, he wrote, "I have never believed that any person has a right to give speeches or engage in demonstrations where he pleases and when he pleases."[14] According to his interpretation of the evidence, the armbands had indeed taken some students' minds off their schoolwork. The protest had roused their emotions and focused their attention on the Vietnam War. Black warned of "a new revolutionary era of permissiveness" that the courts were ushering in.[15] Somewhat sarcastically, he declared:

> This case ... wholly without constitutional reasons in my judgment, subjects all the public schools in the country to the whims and caprices of the loudest-mouthed, but maybe not their brightest students. I, for one, am not fully persuaded that school pupils are wise enough, even with this Court's expert help from Washington, to run the 23,390 public schools in our 50 States.[16]

Black supported the school district all the way. Before a school rule was invalidated, he believed the appellants should have to prove that school officials did not have the interests of the entire school at heart. No one in the *Tinker* v. *Des Moines* case denied that administrators had tried to do what they thought was best.

The Appellants Speak Out

Although John, Christopher, and Mary Beth had been uncertain of the Supreme Court outcome, they had never doubted the rightness of their cause. Two months after the ruling and one year after protesters at Columbia University in New York took over an administration building, Mary Beth wrote an article for a magazine called *Youth* that was published by the Episcopal Church and the United Church of Christ. Her opposition to the war had grown steadily over the years, and she had become deeply disillusioned by political events. She said that black armbands were no longer a strong enough symbol to express the anger and frustration that many Americans were feeling.

> People are thinking that the Vietnam War is just one bad product of a basically corrupt society. People are not content to mourn silently for Vietnam's dead. They want to act in a way that will get to the basis of a government that would carry on such a war, a government that drafts boys to fight and die unwillingly in it, and that starves its poor to pay for it.[17]

Around the time Mary Beth published her article, John also expressed his vision for the future. Like his sister, he wasted few words in coming to the point:

> This decision [*Tinker* v. *Des Moines*] comes at a time when many Americans are afraid of students. . . . It is ironic . . . that they should think that by claiming certain rights we were in some way destructive of the educational system. . . . If school systems cannot . . . provide students with the rights to which they are entitled, then they will be changed, and should be. . . . The Armband Case should provide a . . . springboard for further students' rights. I believe that this is in the best interest of our country and of the democratic system as a whole.[18]

Through the years, John, Christopher, and Mary Beth would all do their part to champion freedom of speech.

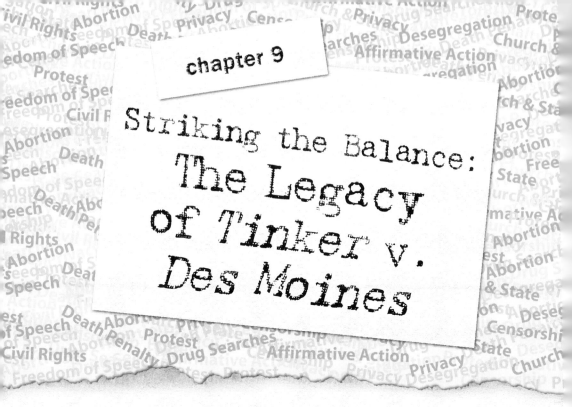

chapter 9

Striking the Balance: The Legacy of Tinker v. Des Moines

In some ways, *Tinker* v. *Des Moines* did provide the springboard that John was hoping for. In 2006, Melvin Wulf, the ACLU lawyer who helped write the appellants' brief, said that *Tinker* v. *Des Moines* was "a major victory for freedom of speech for high school students. It has survived the decades and empowered students to speak out on issues of public importance if they choose to do so."[1] Three basic tenets had been established by the *Tinker* ruling: (1) Students or minors (those under age eighteen) were persons under the law. (2) Schools were required to respect students' constitutional rights. (3) A student's right to freedom of expression could be denied if it caused "substantial disorder or invasion of the rights of others."[2] The courts have used the *Tinker* standard when considering hundreds of free speech and symbolic free speech issues.[3] These include the right to demonstrate, freedom of expression in school publications, library censorship, dress codes, and the right to conduct prayer meetings in public schools.

Speech Plus

According to one analyst, Thomas Flygare, *Tinker v. Des Moines* "ushered in the student rights movement of the 1970s."[4] For several years after the ruling, courts tended to lean toward the students' side in cases that pitted them against school authorities.

Free speech, however, would not be allowed to disrupt the educational process. This became apparent in a federal district court ruling in 1972, *Gebert* v. *Hoffman.* Thirty-six high school students had been suspended for staging a sit-in during and after school. Refusing to move, they didn't attend classes and didn't leave the building after school hours were over.

The students felt their free speech was at stake. Words are not the only way that people communicate. Hairstyle, dress, and general demeanor can all be used to convey a message. When communication is made nonverbally, it is known as *speech plus*.[5] The students were expressing their views through actions instead of words. Did the First Amendment give them the right to do this?

In reaching its decision, the district court relied solely on the "conduct of the demonstrators and not the reaction of the audience."[6] If other students taunted the protesters or even became violent, the students who engaged in the sit-in would not be held responsible.

In spite of this, however, the court did not find in favor of the protesters. Schools are allowed to make rules about student attire and conduct. The students in _Gebert_ v. _Hoffman_ had broken an important school rule that said they had to attend class. This disrupted the entire purpose of the school.

New Jersey v. T.L.O.

Twenty years after John, Christopher, and Mary Beth donned black armbands, another important case came to the Supreme Court. Although it did not concern free speech, it raised important issues about the constitutional rights of children. A fourteen-year-old girl with the initials T.L.O. had been caught smoking outside the girls' restroom at Piscataway High School in New Jersey. Without her permission, the assistant principal, Theodore Choplick, had searched her purse. He found a package of cigarettes, rolling paper for tobacco, and some marijuana. There was also evidence that she planned to sell marijuana to other students. Choplick proceeded to call the police and turned over the results of his search. T.L.O. was charged in juvenile court.

T.L.O.'s lawyer claimed there was a problem with the evidence obtained by Choplick. The Fourth Amendment to the Constitution forbids "unreasonable" searches and seizures. Police cannot search someone's house or car or examine their personal belongings without just cause. If they feel they have a valid reason, they are required to get a warrant. According to T.L.O.'s lawyer, the vice principal had no right to examine her purse. Her constitutional rights had been violated. Any evidence he found should be deemed inadmissible in court.

The Supreme Court disagreed. Writing the majority opinion, Justice Byron R. White declared that requiring a search warrant "would unduly interfere with the swift and informal disciplinary procedures needed in schools."[7] Despite the *Tinker* ruling, the Court was saying that students did not have the same Fourth Amendment rights as adults.[8] They could be searched at school if a teacher suspected they had broken a rule. "Freedom from search and seizure" was apparently a right that students did shed at the schoolhouse gate after all.

Bethel v. Fraser

One year later, the Supreme Court considered another student case that did concern freedom of expression. In 1983, a student named Jeff Kuhlman was running for vice president at Bethel High School in Pierce County, Washington. At the preelection assembly, Jeff's friend, Matt Fraser, made a campaign speech for him that used sexually suggestive language. Some of the students appeared confused or embarrassed. Many of the other six hundred students in the audience laughed and hooted or gestured rudely. School officials were not amused. Bethel High School had a rule that prohibited any behavior that disrupted the educational process. This included "the use of obscene, profane language or gestures."[9] Matt was suspended for three days, and his name was taken off the list of candidates to speak at graduation.

Matt and his family felt that his right to free speech guaranteed by the First Amendment had been violated. Bringing suit against the school district, Matt's lawyers cited *Tinker* v. *Des Moines.* Two lower courts agreed, holding that Matt's suspension was unlawful. School officials decided to appeal.

The Supreme Court found important differences between Matt's situation and that of John, Christopher, and Mary Beth. No political views were involved. It was a matter of whether school officials had a right to forbid the use of inappropriate language in public speeches.[10] On July 7, 1986, in a 7–2 decision, the Court concluded that they did. Chief Justice Warren Burger wrote the majority opinion:

> Surely it is a highly appropriate function of public school education to prohibit the use of vulgar and offensive terms in public discourse. ... Nothing in the Constitution prohibits the states from insisting that certain modes of expression are inappropriate and subject to sanctions [penalties]. The determination of what manner of speech in the classroom or in school assembly is inappropriate properly rests with the school board.[11]

The ruling in *Bethel* v. *Fraser* gave schools more power over student speech than Justice John Stevens and Justice Thurgood Marshall thought was appropriate. Both dissenting justices agreed that schools had the right to set standards for appropriate speech. However, they did not agree that Matt's speech interrupted education or even violated the school's rule. According to Stevens, "a strong presumption in favor of free expression should apply whenever an issue of this kind is arguable." Marshall phrased the same belief differently: "Where speech is involved, we may not unquestioningly accept a teacher's or an administrator's assertion that certain pure speech interfered with education."[12]

But the *Bethel* ruling affirmed the right of the schools to make such assertions and act on them. Although students could still express their views, their free speech was subject to more limits than formerly.

Hazelwood School District v. Kuhlmeier

Perhaps the case that did the most to weaken the precedent set by _Tinker_ v. _Des Moines_ was _Hazelwood School District_ v. _Kulhmeier._ This concerned the 1983 censorship of _Spectrum,_ a school newspaper. Several students at Hazelwood East High School in St. Louis, Missouri, had written articles on subjects their teacher considered controversial— divorce and teen pregnancy. The article on divorce named three students, giving their accounts of why their parents had separated. The author of the pregnancy article also gave personal information about three girls who had become pregnant. But she wrote, "All names have been changed to keep the identity of these girls a secret."[13]

Substitute journalism teacher Howard Emerson felt uneasy when he read the articles. He turned the matter over to the principal, Robert Reynolds, who also questioned whether the articles were appropriate for the paper. Even though their names were not given, the principal knew who the pregnant girls were, and he felt certain that other people would be able to identify them too. Reynolds also believed that the article on divorce was unfair to the parents of the students who had been interviewed. He felt that they should have had a chance to tell their side of the story. In view of these problems, Reynolds decided that the articles should not be published.

Three students involved with the articles decided to bring their case to court. Cathy Kuhlmeier, Leslie Smart, and Leanne

Cathy Kuhlmeier holds a copy of Spectrum, *the school newspaper that was censored by the principal because he objected to some of the articles.*

Tippett believed the censored pieces broached important subjects and that their classmates had a right to read about them. Another issue was at stake as well—the First Amendment rights of the authors and the newspaper staff. Didn't the Constitution guarantee journalists the right to present factual information on any topic? Only the courts could answer that question. The students decided to file a lawsuit.

A federal district court found in favor of the school district, but that ruling was overturned on appeal. Quoting the *Tinker* case, the appellate court stated that the censored material would not "disrupt classwork, give rise to substantial disorder, or invade the rights of others."[14] Naturally, school officials were disappointed by this reversal. They decided to appeal their case to the Supreme Court.

All three students had graduated by the time the Court issued its ruling on January 13, 1988. In delivering the opinion of the Court, Justice White recalled the *Tinker* precedent that students do not "shed their constitutional rights to freedom of speech or expression at the schoolhouse gate."[15] However, he also weighed the finding from *Bethel v. Fraser* that First Amendment rights of young people in schools "are not automatically coextensive with the rights of adults in other settings."[16] Just as they had earlier in *Bethel,* the justices found that the *Tinker* standard did not apply to the *Hazelwood* case. John and Mary Beth Tinker and Christopher Eckhardt had a right to express their political views. School officials had no authority over their beliefs. However, teachers do have authority over what goes into the school newspaper. Anything that appears in a school-sponsored publication seems to have the official approval of the administrators, the Court said.

Spectrum was published as part of the journalism class curriculum. Because of this, the school had greater responsibility over its contents than over the free expression of individual students. Justice White wrote:

> In sum, we cannot reject as unreasonable Principal Reynolds' conclusion that neither the pregnancy article nor the divorce article was suitable for publication in *Spectrum*. Reynolds could reasonably have concluded that the students who had written and edited these articles had not sufficiently mastered those portions of the Journalism II curriculum that pertained to the treatment of controversial issues and personal attacks, the need to protect the privacy of individuals whose most intimate concerns are to be revealed in the newspaper and "the legal, moral and ethical restrictions imposed upon journalists within [a] school community" that includes adolescent subjects and readers.[17]

The majority of the justices thought that the school's right to control the content of the newspaper was more important than the students' right to free speech. However, Justice William Brennan noted that the school board had a policy to "not restrict free expression or diverse viewpoints within the rules of responsible journalism."[18] He believed that the principal had violated this policy by censoring articles "that neither disrupt[ed] classwork nor invad[ed] the rights of others."[19] In a scathing dissent that was joined by Justices Harry Blackmun and Thurgood Marshall, Brennan recalled the same words from *Tinker* v. *Des Moines* that Justice White had used in the majority opinion:

> The Court opens its analysis in this case by purporting to reaffirm *Tinker*'s time-tested proposition that public school students "do not 'shed their constitutional rights to freedom of speech or expression at the schoolhouse gate.'" . . . That is an ironic introduction to an opinion that denudes [robs] high school students of much of the First Amendment protection that *Tinker* itself prescribed. . . . The Court today "teach[es] youth to discount important principles of our government as mere platitudes."[20]

Dan Johnston, who had argued the *Tinker* case before the Supreme Court, was also deeply disappointed by the Hazelwood ruling. "All my life," he told *The Wall Street Journal*, "I've been saying proudly I was the lawyer in *Tinker*. I'd built a statue to myself in my mind. But the Supreme Court melted down my statue when it decided *Hazelwood*."[21]

Looking Back Thirty Years Later

Although the *Tinker* ruling still stands as a safeguard to student free speech, the *Fraser* and *Hazelwood* cases put limits on that freedom. Thirty years after the Supreme Court ruled in favor of the armband protest, several of the key participants talked about the climate for student rights in 1999. Despite later Supreme Court decisions, Christopher Eckhardt considered *Tinker* an enduring landmark decision. He hoped that it showed young people of a new generation the "importance of nonviolence and of nonviolent protest."[22]

Reflecting on *Fraser* and on *Hazelwood,* John Tinker remarked that he wasn't too worried about the limits they define "because *Fraser* was not about pure political speech and the *Hazelwood* case involved the school newspaper—both are distinguishable."[23]

Dan Johnston, however, was not so optimistic. "The real question is whether the present-day Supreme Court would reach the same decision," Johnston said. "I think the answer is probably not." He also admitted, "The issues today are a lot tougher."[24]

Protesting in the Wake of 9/11

The question of where to draw the line between student rights and school authority is very much alive. Several disputes have occurred between school administrators and students who protested the war in Iraq. One involved a fifteen-year-old sophomore named Katie Sierra. On October 23, 2001, Katie asked the principal of Sissonville High School in West Virginia if she could start an anarchy club. Traditionally, anarchists have been people who did not believe in structured government. Sometimes they want to overthrow the established order. Katie made it clear that her views were different. "This anarchist club will not tolerate hate or violence," she said.[25] Principal Forrest Mann did not give Katie permission to form the club.

Katie's request came barely six weeks after terrorist attacks had destroyed the World Trade Center in New York and damaged the Pentagon in Washington, D.C. A wave of patriotism had swept the country. But Katie did not like the way people were reacting to the tragedy of 9/11. She was appalled when the United States began bombing Afghanistan.

Even before the terrorist attacks, Katie had used marker pens to write her opinions on the T-shirts she wore to school. Now she added more statements. One of her T-shirts read sarcastically, "When I saw the dead and dying children in Afghanistan, I felt a newly recovered sense of national security."[26] Katie also wore shirts that made fun of exaggerated patriotism, although she expressed a love for her country. Finally, Principal Mann forbade her to wear the controversial T-shirts. He believed they were disruptive. Mann also suspended her from school for three days for showing flyers about the anarchy club to other students. An angry Katie wasted no time that afternoon. She contacted the ACLU for advice on how to fight for her rights.

Represented by two lawyers connected with the ACLU, Katie lost her first round in court. A circuit judge upheld the principal's ban on her T-shirts.

Students' right to protest is under dispute following the terrorist attacks of September 11, 2001. These high school students in Fort Wayne, Indiana, are taking part in a demonstration against the Iraq war.

Disappointed but determined, Katie tore up some black fabric and went to school the next day wearing an armband. News of her battle spread. A week after she lost her case, Kate got an e-mail from fifty-one-year-old John Tinker. He pledged his support and told her to keep fighting.[27] He even came to meet her. Sponsored by the West Virginia ACLU, Katie Sierra and John Tinker embarked on an educational program called "Tinker Days" in 2002. They visited several colleges and told about their experiences and encouraged students to become involved in important issues. "It's important to stand up for what you believe in. It just feels like the right thing to do," said Katie.[28]

On July 8, 2002, Katie's case came to trial again. This time the jury ruled that Katie did have a right to start an anarchy club on campus to discuss her views. However, the jury agreed with Principal Mann that her T-shirts were disruptive—especially in light of current events. Despite this, Katie's lawyer, Roger Forman, felt that his client had won the most important part of the case. "We won the big free-speech issue," he said. "Post-[September 11], a jury in Kanawha County said, 'Don't mess with our speech.' I think that's very signficant."[29]

Barber v. Dearborn

Another incident, which occurred in Dearborn, Michigan, in 2003, also reveals the tension between free speech and the special needs of the school environment. On February 17 of that year, a student named Bretton (Brett) Barber came to school wearing a T-shirt with a picture of President George W. Bush and the words "International Terrorist." Asked by Vice Principal Michael Shelton to remove the shirt or wear it inside out, Brett refused. He opted to go home instead. "The shirt was meant to emphasize the message 'no war,'" explained Brett. "High school can be a pretty apathetic place. I had hoped to generate some discussion about what was then the brewing war in Iraq."[30]

Principal Judith Coebly and Vice Principal Shelton were more concerned with the possibility of students clashing. Almost one third of the students at Dearborn High School were Arab. Some of their families came from Iraq. Many of them opposed the dictator Saddam Hussein and believed that the United States should attack Iraq. They might react violently to Brett's message about President Bush.[31] The principal also feared that the students' emotions would be volatile because the terrorist alert was at a high level.

Backed by the ACLU, Brett decided to go to court. John Tinker heard about the impending case on a radio talk show while he was driving to speak at a school in Chicago. He pulled over to the side of the road and whipped out his cell phone. "Of course, [Brett] has a right to wear his T-shirt," he told the talk-show host.[32] Later that night, John offered Brett encouragement over the phone.

A federal judge, Patrick J. Duggan, sided with Barber. He did not believe that the T-shirt had caused problems or that the school had sufficient reason to fear disruption. He wrote:

> The courts have never declared that the school yard is an inappropriate place for political debate. In fact, as the *Tinker* Court and other courts have

emphasized, students benefit when school officials provide an environment where they can openly express their diverging viewpoints and when they learn to tolerate the opinions of others.[33]

"Speak Out"

Free speech issues don't always have to do with national politics. In June 2004, seventeen-year-old Tiffany Schley, valedictorian at the High School of Legal Studies in Brooklyn, gave her graduation speech.

Lots of things needed improvement at Tiffany's school. As editor of her school paper, a member of the student council, and the chairperson of the yearbook committee, Tiffany was used to speaking honestly. In her speech, she mentioned crowded classrooms, too few textbooks, and a lack of communication between students and school officials. She also pointed out that the school had had four principals in four years.[34] Whatever else she planned to say was lost. An angry assistant principal turned off her microphone.

Graduates were supposed to pick up their diplomas the day after the ceremony. When Tiffany arrived to get her diploma, she was told that her speech had disrupted the graduation and that she could not receive her diploma until she apologized. Then security guards escorted Tiffany and her mother out of the school building.

Tiffany Schley is shown (second from right) with family members and community leaders before a ceremony at which she was given her diploma and a special award.

No lawsuit was ever filed, but people all over New York were outraged. "What bozo tried to hold back a diploma in a country where freedom of speech is so prized, I don't know," exclaimed Mayor Michael Bloomberg.[35]

Eventually the school district had Tiffany's diploma sent to her home. Black New Yorkers for Educational Excellence (BNYEE) felt the occasion demanded a bit more ceremony. They organized a special event with noted African-American educator Dr. Adelaide Sanford giving Tiffany her diploma. Tiffany also received a valedictorian plaque and BNYEE's Harriet Tubman–Ida B. Wells award.

"Although people may have been offended by my speech," Tiffany said on another occasion, "I stand by what I say because it was the truth, and the truth sometimes hurts."[36] Featured on a Sunday talk show, Tiffany encouraged other teenagers: "Speak out."[37]

The Appellants Today

Besides its national legacy, the *Tinker* case has left a profound impact on the lives of all those who were involved. "As a child, I saw the system work in *Tinker* v. *Des Moines*," said Christopher Eckhardt.[38] Recent difficulties have not changed his views. In 2001, Christopher was sentenced to prison for a nonviolent crime. Released after serving almost five years, he is still determined to establish his innocence. He is also writing a book about his experiences in prison and working as an energy consultant.

Christopher states:

> I think we have a glorious country. I love America. Yes, there are problems, but the fact of the matter is we have the right to complain. I have the right to say that what they did to me was wrong. I appreciate freedom much more now, having been through the degradation of prison.[39]

John Tinker, still deeply concerned with free speech issues, enjoys visiting schools to talk about

Tinker v. *Des Moines*. He encourages students to speak their minds. To help people keep informed on current affairs, he maintains a Web site that is an encyclopedia of world events. Although his own position remains liberal, John Tinker is called on to support students of all views in disputes involving free speech. "I care less about a person's politics than I do about the democratic process," he explains.[40] What is important to him is that students think deeply about the issues and stand up for their beliefs. "I think it's great that conservative students can make use of our case," he says, "and that religious students use our case."[41]

Like her brother, Mary Beth Tinker is deeply involved in contemporary issues and outspoken in her views. Forty years after the Vietnam War protest in which her brother and mother marched, Mary Beth joined a huge demonstration in Washington, D.C., against the war in Iraq. She was not surprised to see many students and young people among the protesters. A family nurse-practitioner who works mostly with children, Mary Beth believes that young people have an important role to play in society. When she visits schools, she likes to ask the questions: "Are things fair? What should be changed? Kids seem to have a natural sense of what's fair and right," she says.[42]

The conflict between free speech and an orderly environment in the schools is far from over. New situations are bound to arise that will test the boundaries. However, most people agree with Mary Beth that it is important for deeply committed young people to ask questions, challenge authority, and say what is on their minds.

Mary Beth Tinker declared in April 2005:

> The relevance of [*Tinker*] today "is that we have many issues that we need to work on to improve our country and our world. . . . To resolve those problems in a peaceful way, we need the involvement of students. There have never been major changes in the world without the active involvement of young people."[43]

chapter 10

Moot Court: Your Turn to Debate

This chapter tells you how to take part in a mock judicial proceeding of your own.[1] Such an exercise is called "moot court." Participants in a moot court dramatize a hypothetical (fictitious) or real case that went before an appeals court or the Supreme Court. The purpose of these higher courts is to rule on a lower court's decision. Appeal courts are different from lower court trials. No witnesses testify, just as no witnesses are called in a Supreme Court case. Instead, the justices must decide if the court below made a mistake.

In a moot court, the players take the parts of the attorneys and justices. They also become clerks and journalists. As attorneys, they do research, write briefs, and argue legal issues. As justices, they rule on the validity of these arguments. These activities sharpen writing and debate skills.

Taking part in a moot court is a fun way to learn how a real court case unfolds. Try a moot activity with your class or club. Here's how.

Step 1: Assign Roles

Here are the roles you will need to fill:

◇ Judges. If the group is large enough, have nine justices like the Supreme Court has. Otherwise, have a panel of three appellate court judges. The person chosen as chief justice will run the proceeding. The judges will question the attorneys as they argue their positions. Then the judges will write and deliver the final ruling. The court's majority opinion is the position agreed upon by a majority of the panel. Individual justices may choose to issue concurring or dissenting opinions of their own.

◇ Two or more court clerks. Working closely with the justices, the clerks prepare five or more questions to ask the attorneys during oral arguments. Judicial clerks also do research to help the justices in writing their opinions.

◇ A team of two or more attorneys for the appellant (the party that appealed the decision). They argue that the lower court ruling was wrong.

◇ A team of two or more attorneys for the appellee (the party who won the case in the lower court). They believe the court below ruled correctly.

◇ A designated spokesperson for each side who will present the argument. (Although there is only one spokesperson, any lawyer on the team can answer questions from the justices). Attorneys address the major issues and put forth the most persuasive arguments for their side.

◇ Two or more reporters. They interview the attorneys before the case, write news stories, and report the final ruling.

◇ The bailiff, who will call the court to order and time each side's oral arguments.

Step 2: Prepare Your Case: Isobel Williams v. Mayfield School District

Part 1: Gather Information
The case you will hear and decide is based on *Tinker* v. *Des Moines*.

The situation:

(1) Appellant's view:
The appellant, sixteen-year-old Isobel Williams, is a junior at Albert Einstein High School. From the time she was very young, she has heard her parents discuss current events and the violence that exists throughout the world. She knows they are pacifists, but they have never tried to impose

Students in Maine take part in a mock trial. Judicial exercises like this are fun as well as being good for research, reasoning, and debating skills.

their views on her. Instead, they have encouraged her to listen to the news, to question what she hears, and to think for herself.

Isobel has decided that wars create more problems than they solve. She is horrified by the loss of life and feels strongly that no young man or woman should ever be put in the position of having to kill or be killed. When the United States went to war in Iraq, Isobel felt the need to protest. She designed her own T-shirt, which read: "Stop the Murder in Iraq Now."

When Isobel wore her shirt to school, she attracted a great deal of attention. Some classmates were angered; others told her there was nothing she could do to stop the war. A few students supported her, and one asked where he could get a T-shirt like hers. Although several students made threatening remarks, Isobel was not frightened. In history class, her shirt set off a heated discussion, which lasted most of the period.

During the afternoon, one of her teachers reported the T-shirt to the principal, Sarah Wilson. Summoning Isobel to her office, Wilson said that shirt violated the school's dress code. When Isobel objected, the principal explained that the shirt was offensive to the majority of the students and teachers—especially the use of the word "murder." She also told Isobel that this was a time to support her country, not to criticize it. Principal Wilson gave Isobel another T-shirt and asked her to put it on over her own. Isobel refused. The principal then said she had no choice but to suspend Isobel from school.

Isobel felt that she had been picked on because her views were not popular with the student body. But didn't she have the same right to express her opinion as someone who supported the war? After discussing it with her parents, Isobel called the local branch of the ACLU. Several lawyers believed that her right to free speech had been violated. Isobel decided to purse the matter in court.

(2) Appellee's View

Sarah Wilson believes that her first duty is to the student body as a whole. She has the responsibility (1) to ensure the safety of all the students, and (2) to maintain an environment conducive to learning. A T-shirt equating the war in Iraq with murder is detrimental to both these goals, Wilson believes.

Although Wilson sympathizes with Isobel's view, she cannot allow one student to disrupt the entire school. Patriotism is running high at Albert Einstein High School. Several students have family members serving in the military. They could view Isobel's T-shirt as a slur on their loved ones. Ms. Wilson has received several reports of students who were offended. She is especially troubled to learn that two students labeled Isobel a traitor and taunted her. The safety of the students cannot be guaranteed in such an emotionally charged atmosphere.

Isobel's apparel also endangers Ms. Wilson's second responsibility. By taking her classmates' minds off their studies and focusing them on the war, Isobel is interfering with the learning process. When students are angry or combative, they cannot focus on math or literature or science. Ms. Wilson fears that Isobel's protest against the war will lead to counterprotests. The situation will escalate until the whole purpose of the educational system is thwarted. More demonstrating than learning will take place in the school. Although Isobel has a right to state her views, she has no right to undermine the orderly functioning of the school.

Isobel's case goes all the way to the Supreme Court. The two sides are made up of the following people:

⬦ Isobel (the appellant), her parents, and their lawyers. They must prove that Isobel's right to freedom of speech under the First Amendment has been denied. They must also show that the way she chose to express her views did not disrupt the school or infringe on the rights of other students.

⬦ The school principal, Sarah Wilson, other administrators at Albert Einstein High

School, and several officials in the school district (the appellees). Their job is to prove that Isobel's T-shirt presented a danger to safety and order in the school and that it distracted students from learning.

Part 2: Write Your Briefs

A legal brief is a written presentation of your argument. Brainstorm with the lawyers on your team. Decide which are your best and which are your weakest arguments.

You may want to divide up the arguments among the members of your team. If so, be sure to work together as you write your final brief. Otherwise, your arguments may be choppy or not sound logically convincing.

Use the arguments above as suggestions and think of arguments of your own that might be convincing to the court. Each team should also look to past Supreme Court decisions (as presented in this book). Establishing legal precedent (showing how the desired outcome follows logically from past decisions) helps to strengthen the case. The lawyers should also discuss what a decision against them would mean for students' rights and for the educational system.

In real life, court rules spell out what briefs must contain. Use these rules for your moot court activity.

1. The cover page should have the case name, *Isobel Williams* v. *Mayfield School District,*

and say whether it is the case for the appellant or the appellee. List the lawyers' names.

2. The text of the brief should have these sections:

   A. Statement of the issue for review: What question is before the court?

   B. Statement of the case: What is this case about? How did the trial court rule?

   C. Statement of the facts: Briefly describe the facts relevant to the case.

   D. Summary of the arguments: Sum up your argument in 150 words or less.

   E. Argument: Spell out the legal arguments that support your side. You can split this into sections with sub-headings for each part. Include references to cases or authorities that help your side.

   F. Conclusion: Ask the court to rule in your favor.

3. Real appeals briefs may be thirty pages long. Limit your brief to no more than five typed pages, double-spaced, or about 1,250 words. If possible, type on a computer. Otherwise, write very neatly.

4. On an agreed-upon date, each team gives the other a copy of its brief. Each judge gets a copy too. So does the teacher if you are doing this in class. Be sure that each team member also keeps a copy of the brief.

In real life, lawyers often prepare reply briefs. They must answer points made by the other side. You do not need to do this. But be ready to answer points that the other side will raise in oral arguments.

Part 3: Prepare for Oral Argument
Each side receives up to fifteen minutes to argue its case. Choose one or two students from each side to present the most important arguments to the judges. Those chosen should practice their speeches so they can make the strongest argu- ments in the set amount of time.

As the lawyers put together their arguments, the journalists quietly visit both sides and take notes. They write the lead paragraph of a newspaper story about the case, explaining the major issues and the impact the decision is expected to have. These paragraphs can be posted on the bulletin board.

The judges read and discuss all the briefs before hearing oral arguments. They review past cases and decide what questions they would like to ask each set of lawyers. The clerks review the case with the judges and may suggest questions.

Step 3: Hold the Oral Arguments

Part 1: Assemble the Participants
◇ The judges sit in a panel at the head of the room. This is called the bench. They should

not enter until the bailiff calls the court to order. A speaking podium or lectern faces the bench.

◊ The appellant's (Isobel's) team of attorneys sits at one side, facing the judges.

◊ The appellee's (school district's) team sits at the opposite side, also facing the judges.

◊ The reporters sit at the back.

◊ As the judges enter, the bailiff calls the court to order: "Oyez [pronounced 'oy-yay'; means 'Hear ye']! Oyez! Oyez! The _____ Court of the United States in now in session with the Honorable Chief Justice _____ presiding. All will stand and remain standing until the judges are seated and the Chief Justice has asked all present to be seated."

Part 2: Present the Case

◊ The Chief Justice calls the case and asks whether the parties are ready. Each team's spokesperson answers "Yes."

◊ The appellants' spokesperson approaches the podium and says, "May it please the court." Then he or she begins the oral arguments. Judges interrupt when they wish to ask a question. The attorneys pause to answer. Do not get flustered if a judge interrupts with a question. Answer honestly and move on.

◊ The appellee's team presents its arguments.

◊ Each side gets fifteen minutes to present its arguments. If the appellant's team wishes, it can save five minutes of its time to rebut the appellee's argument. If so, the spokesperson should inform the court before sitting down.

◇ After oral arguments, the bailiff has everyone rise as the judges retire to their chambers to debate their decision.

◇ At this time, reporters may interview lawyers for the parties and begin working on their articles.

◇ After a set amount of time, the judges return. The Chief Justice announces the ruling that will affect the First Amendment rights of students everywhere.

Step 4: Publish and Report the Decision

After a few days, the court issues its majority opinion in written form. In addition, dissenting justices may issue opinions and individual justices may issue their own concurring opinions. At this time, the reporters' stories are made available.

Your moot court proceedings are now over. When a real Supreme Court case concludes, however, its impact lasts forever unless a different ruling supersedes it. The *Tinker* case affected every school in the country. Thanks to the determination of three courageous students, young people know they are free to express their opinions in a respectful, nondisruptive manner.

1. Justice Abe Fortas stated in the majority opinion of *Tinker* v. *Des Moines*: "In our system, state-operated schools may not be enclaves of totalitarianism." What does this mean? Do you think the appellants in this case were being punished for their beliefs?

2. Do principals have the right to restrict the opinions that students may openly support at school? For example, should students be allowed to show approval for hate or terrorist organizations?

3. The students and the school administrators disagreed on whether or not the armband protest caused a disruption. What do you think would constitute a serious disturbance of school? Do you agree with the school district that different standards should be used in judging a disruption in school and a disruption in another public setting?

4. Do you think that high school students should have the same legal rights as adults? Why or why not?

5. In *Hazelwood* v. *Kuhlmeier*, the Supreme Court noted that a school has more responsibility for

what is published in the student newspaper than the views students express in the hallways or the classrooms. Do you agree? Should students be able to express any view in their newspaper? Why or why not?

6. Are there situations when one group's exercise of student free speech may harm or conflict with the rights of other students? How should such problems be handled?

7. What do you think is more important, the responsibility of school officials to protect the learning environment or the rights of students to express their views freely? Why?

Chapter Notes

Chapter 1. "Surrounded by the Antiwar Movement"

1. Author phone interview with John Tinker, July 14, 2005.

2. "Throng of 20,000 Marches in Protest of Vietnam War," *The Washington Post, Times Herald* (1959–1973); November 28, 1965; ProQuest Historical Newspapers, *The Washington Post*.

3. John W. Johnson, *The Struggle for Student Rights: Tinker v. Des Moines and the 1960s* (Lawrence, Kansas: University Press of Kansas, 1997), p. 13.

4. Author phone interview with John Tinker, July 14, 2005.

5. Johnson, p. 10.

6. Author phone interview with John Tinker, August 1, 2005.

7. Lorena Jeanne Tinker, armband notes, *Tinker v. Des Moines*, 1965, <http://schema-root.org/region/americas/north_america/usa/government/judicial_branch/supreme_court/decisions/schools/tinker_v._des_moines/~jft/ljt.notes.1965.html> (July 29, 2005).

8. Johnson, p. 6.

Chapter 2. The Right to Protest

1. Author phone interview with John Tinker, July 14, 2005.

2. Ibid.

3. Author phone interview with Christopher Eckhardt, May 25, 2006.

4. John W. Johnson, *The Struggle for Student Rights: Tinker v. Des Moines and the 1960s* (Lawrence, Kansas: University Press of Kansas, 1997), p. 26.

5. Author phone interview with Lorena Jeanne Tinker, October 12, 2005.

6. Author phone interview with Christopher Eckhardt, May 25, 2006.

7. Johnson, p. 17.

8. Ibid.

9. Ibid., p. 18.

10. Author phone interview with Mary Beth Tinker, October 21, 2005.

11. Lorena Jeanne Tinker, armband notes, 1965, *Tinker v. Des Moines,* <http://schema-root.org/region/americas/north_america/usa/government/judicial_branch/sup...> (July 29, 2005).

12. Ibid.

13. Ibid.

14. Author phone interview with John Tinker, July 17, 2005.

15. Ibid.

16. Ibid.

17. Ibid.

18. Ibid.

19. Lorena Jeanne Tinker, armband notes.

20. Johnson, p. 36.

21. Ibid., p. 46.

Chapter 3. Hawks and Doves

1. Stanley Karnow, *Vietnam: A History: The First Complete Account of Vietnam at War* (New York: Viking Press, 1983), pp. 223–224.

2. Ibid., p. 224.

3. Ibid., pp. 370–371.

4. "Episode 11: Vietnam—Gulf of Tonkin Resolution," *CNN Interactive,* n.d., <http://www.cnn.com/SPECIALS/cold.war/episodes/11/documents/tonkin/> (February 20, 2006).

5. "A Look Down That Long Road," *Time Archive*, February 19, 1965, <http://www.time.com/time/archive/printout/0,23657,905234,00.html> (February 20, 2006).

6. Leo J. Daugherty and Gregory Louis Mattson, *Nam: A Photographic History* (New York: Barnes & Noble Books, 2001), p. 40.

7. Ibid., p. 48.

8. William L. Langer, ed., *An Encyclopedia of World History: Ancient, Medieval, and Modern*, 5th ed. (Boston: Houghton Mifflin Company, 1980), p. 1327.

9. "Throng of 20,000 Marches in Protest of Vietnam War," *The Washington Post, Times Herald* (1959–1973); November 28, 1965; Pro Quest Historical Newspapers, *The Washington Post* (1877–1988).

Chapter 4. Constitutional Rights for Young People

1. Lawrence M. Friedman, "Limited Monarchy: The Rise and Fall of Student Rights" in *School Days, Rule Days: The Legalization and Regulation of Education*, eds. David L. Kirp and Donald N. Jensen (Philadelphia and London: The Falmer Press, a member of the Taylor & Francis Group, 1986), p. 240.

2. Robert Wheeler Lane, *Beyond the Schoolhouse Gate: Free Speech and the Inculcation of Values* (Philadelphia: Temple University Press, 1995), p. 17.

3. Ibid., p. 18.

4. Friedman, p. 241.

5. "Introduction to the Court Opinion on the West Virginia Board of Education v. Barnette Case. Source: 319 U.S. 624 (1943)," *Basic Readings in U.S. Democracy*, n.d., <http://usinfo.state.gov/usa/infousa/facts/democrac/46.htm> (February 20, 2006).

6. *In Re Gault*, 387 U.S. 1; 18 L. Ed. 2d 527; 87 S. Ct. 1428 (1967).

7. Ibid.

8. Lane, p. 75.

Chapter 5. Taking a Stand for Free Speech

1. John W. Johnson, *The Struggle for Student Rights: Tinker v. Des Moines and the 1960s* (Lawrence, Kansas: University Press of Kansas, 1997), p. 48.

2. Author phone interview with John Tinker, July 14, 2005.

3. Author phone interview with Lorena Tinker, October 12, 2005.

4. Author phone interview with Mary Beth Tinker, October 21, 2005.

5. Johnson, p. 57.

6. Ibid., pp. 56–57.

7. Author phone interview with John Tinker, July 14, 2005.

8. Ibid.

9. Ibid.

10. Ibid.

11. Author phone interview with Bruce Clark, May 31, 2006.

12. Johnson, p. 79.

13. Ibid.

14. *Tinker v. Des Moines Independent Community School District* 258 F. Supp. 971 (S.D. Iowa 1966) rev., 393 U.S. 503 (1969).

15. Ibid.

16. Ibid.

17. *Tinker v. Des Moines*, 258 F. Supp. 971.

18. Ibid.

19. Johnson, p. 99.

20. Ibid., p. 102.

21. Author phone interview with John Tinker, August 1, 2005.

22. Ibid.

23. David Hudson, "On 30-year anniversary, Tinker participants look back at landmark case," *freedomforum. org,* February 24, 1999, <http://www. freedomforum.org/templates/document.asp?documentID=10386> (August 13, 2005).

Chapter 6. The Case for the Students

1. Author phone interview with Bruce Clark, May 25, 2006.

2. John W. Johnson, *The Struggle for Student Rights: Tinker* v. *Des Moines and the 1960s* (Lawrence, Kansas: University Press of Kansas, 1997), p. 130.

3. Petitioner's Brief, *Tinker* v. *Des Moines Indep. Cmy. Sch. Dist.,* 393 U.S. 503 (1969) (no. 21).

4. Ibid.

5. Ibid.

6. Ibid.

7. Ibid.

8. Ibid.

9. Ibid.

10. Ibid.

11. Johnson, p. 132.

Chapter 7. The Case for the School District

1. John W. Johnson, *The Struggle for Student Rights: Tinker* v. *Des Moines and the 1960s* (Lawrence Kansas: University Press of Kansas, 1997), p. 138.

2. Ibid.

3. Respondent's Brief, *Tinker* v. *Des Moines Indep. Cmty. Sch. Dist.,* 393 U.S. 503 (1969) (no. 21).

4. Ibid.

5. Ibid.

6. Ibid.

7. Ibid.

8. Ibid.

9. Ibid.

10. Ibid.

Chapter 8. The Supreme Court Decides

1. "*Tinker* v. *Des Moines* Oral Arguments: Transcript," p. 10, <http://schema-root.org/region/americas/north_america/usa/government/judicial_branch/supreme_court/decisions/schools/tinker_v._des_moines/_stacks/oral_argument.html> (July 29, 2005).

2. Ibid., pp. 11–12.

3. Ibid., p. 12.

4. David Hudson, "On 30-year anniversary, Tinker participants look back at landmark case," *freedomforum. org,* February 24, 1999, <http://www.freedomforum.org/templates/document.asp?documentID=10386> (August 13, 2005).

5. Author phone interview with Christopher Eckhardt, May 25, 2006.

6. John W. Johnson, *The Struggle for Student Rights: Tinker* v. *Des Moines and the 1960s* (Lawrence, Kansas: University Press of Kansas, 1997), p. 183.

7. *Tinker* v. *Des Moines School District,* 393 U.S. 503 (1969). Argued November 12, 1968. Decided February 24, 1969.

8. Ibid.

9. Ibid.

10. Ibid.

11. Ibid.

12. Ibid.

13. Ibid.

14. Ibid.

15. Ibid.

16. Ibid.

17. Johnson, p. 185.

18. Ibid., pp. 183, 184.

Chapter 9. Striking the Balance: The Legacy of *Tinker v. Des Moines*

1. Melvin Wulf, e-mail, May 19, 2006.

2. Robert Wheeler Lane, *Beyond the Schoolhouse Gate: Free Speech and the Inculcation of Values* (Philadelphia: Temple University Press, 1995), pp. 76, 77.

3. John W. Johnson, *The Struggle for Student Rights: Tinker v. Des Moines and the 1960s* (Lawrence, Kansas: University Press of Kansas, 1997), p. 207.

4. Lane, 75.

5. Ibid., p. 78.

6. Ibid., p. 79.

7. *New Jersey v. T.L.O.*, 469 U.S. 325 (1985). Argued March 28, 1984. Reargued October 2, 1984. Decided January 15, 1985.

8. Johnson, p. 207.

9. *Bethel School District No. 403 v. Fraser*, 478 U.S. 675 (1986). Argued March 3, 1986. Decided July 7, 1986.

10. Ibid.

11. Ibid.

12. Ibid.

13. Peter Irons, ed., *May It Please the Court: Courts, Kids and the Constitution* (New York: The New Press, 2000), p. 235.

14. Ibid., p. 236.

15. *Hazelwood School District v. Kulhmeier*, 484 U.S. 260 (1988). Argued October 13, 1987. Decided January 13, 1988.

16. Ibid.

17. Ibid.

18. Ibid.

19. Ibid.

20. Ibid.

21. Johnson, p. 210.

22. David Hudson, "On 30-year anniversary, Tinker participants look back at landmark case," _freedomforum. org,_ February 24, 1999, <http://freedomforum.org/ templates/document.asp?documentID=10386> (August 13, 2005).

23. Ibid.

24. Ibid.

25. "Teen anarchist sues school principal," Trial Report, _COURTTV.com,_ September 17, 2002, <http://www.courttv. com/trials/taped/sierra/background ctv.html> (September 19, 2005).

26. Ibid.

27. "John Tinker pledges support for pro-anarchy teen," _freedomforum.org,_ December 4, 2001, <http://www. freedomforum.org/templates/document.asp?documentID= 15460> (August 13, 2005).

28. Christina McGough and Jessica Karmasek, "Tinker Days to focus on freedom of speech," _The Daily Athenaeum,_ February 28, 2002, <http://www.da.wvu.edu/ archives/022802/news/022802,01,01.html> (September 2005).

29. "Jury says W. Va. student can form anarchy club at school: Decision relies on Supreme Court's _Tinker_ ruling promoting student expression," _Student Press Law Center,_ July 17, 2002, <http://www. splc.org/newsflash_archives. asp?id=455&year=2002> (September 19, 2005).

30. "Bretton Barber: When It Comes to Free Speech, He Won't Give You the Shirt Off His Back," _American Civil Liberties Union: Profile Bretton Barber,_ n.d., <http://www. aclu.org/TakeAction.cfm?Id=12954&c=242> (September 19, 2005).

31. _Barber_ v. _Dearborn Public School,_ 286 F. Supp. 2d 847 (E.D. Michigan 2003).

32. Author phone interview with John Tinker, August 1, 2005.

33. *Barber* v. *Dearborn Public School.*

34. Nat Hentoff, "Valedictorian of the Year," *Jewish World Review,* July 20, 2004, <http://www.jewishworld review.com/cols/hentoff072004.asp> (May 18, 2006).

35. Ibid.

36. Donna Lamb, "Valedictorian Denied Diploma After Speaking Truth to Power at High School Graduation," *Global Black News,* July 2, 2004, <http://www. globalblacknews.com/Lamb61.html> (September 20, 2005).

37. Hentoff.

38. Author phone interview with Christopher Eckhardt, May 25, 2006.

39. Ibid.

40. Author phone interview with John Tinker, August 1, 2005.

41. Author phone interview with John Tinker, October 12, 2005.

42. Author phone interview with Mary Beth Tinker, October 21, 2005.

43. Amy Klein, "Student freedoms discussed through landmark decision," *Iowa State Daily, Online Edition,* April 13, 2005, <http://www.iowastatedaily.com/media/ storage/paper818/news/2005/04/13/News/Student. Freedoms.Discussed.Through.Landmark.Decision-1103872.shtml?norewrite200605191529&sourcedomain =www.iowastatedaily.com> (August 13, 2005).

Chapter 10. Moot Court: Your Turn to Debate

1. The material in this chapter is adapted from Millie Aulbur, "Constitutional Issues and Teenagers," *The Missouri Bar,* n.d., <http://www. mobar.org/teach/clesson. htm> (December 10, 2004); Street Law, Inc., and The

Supreme Court Historical Society, "Moot Court Activity," 2002, <http://www.landmarkcases.org> (December 10, 2004); with suggestions from Ron Fridell and Kathiann M. Kowalski.

Glossary

capitalism—An economic system based on free enterprise. The United States has a capitalist economy.

cold war—A period of intense rivalry between capitalism and communism. Many Americans believed that communism had to be defeated at all costs.

communism—A system in which the government, instead of private individuals, controls business. Communism places other restrictions on freedom as well.

doves—People who wanted to stop the war in Vietnam.

Equal Protection Clause—Portion of the Fourteenth Amendment to the Constitution that grants equal protection to all citizens.

First Amendment—First item in the Bill of Rights, which guarantees freedom of speech and freedom of religion to all citizens.

hawks—People who supported the Vietnam War.

pure speech—Views expressed verbally or in writing.

speech plus—Personal expression through such means as hairstyles, dress, and general behavior.

Further Reading

Dudley, William, ed. *Freedom of Speech.* San Diego, Calif.: Greenhaven Press, 2005.

Egendorf, Laura K., ed. *Should There Be Limits to Free Speech?* San Diego, Calif.: Greenhaven Press, 2003.

Hibbert, Adam. *Children's Rights.* North Mankato, Minn.: Sea-to-Sea Publications, 2005.

Isler, Claudia. *The Right to Free Speech.* New York: Rosen Publishing Group, 2001.

Jacobs, Thomas A. *Teens on Trial: Young People Who Challenged the Law—and Changed Your Life.* Minneapolis, Minn.: Free Spirit Publishing, 2000.

Krull, Kathleen. *A Kid's Guide to America's Bill of Rights: Curfews, Censorship, and the 100-Pound Giant.* New York: Avon Books, 1999.

Pendergast, Tom, Sara Pendergast, and John Sousanis. *Constitutional Amendments: From Freedom of Speech to Flag Burning.* Detroit, Mich.: UXL, 2001.

Internet Addresses

Ben's Guide to the U.S. Government for Kids—The Supreme Court
<http://bensguide.gpo.gov/9-12/government/national/scourt.html>

For Kids—National Constitution Center
<http://www.constitutioncenter.org/explore/ForKids/index.shtml>

Online Conversation—*Tinker* v. *Des Moines* School Plaintiffs
<http://www.abanet.org/publiced/lawday/tinker>

Index